<u>Management</u> is the **process** of designing and maintaining an environment in which individuals work together with the aim of achieving
goals **effectively** and **efficiently**.   Or

Management is the process of getting things done with the aim of achieving goals effectively and efficiently

- Definition of management stresses upon **achieving goals, process, effectiveness and efficiency**

- **Goals/objectives/targets/aims:** **Refers to end points towards which all business activities are directed**

<u>**Management as a process**</u>: as it involves a series of inter related functions such as planning, organizing, staffing, directing and controlling

Functions of management (POSDC)

(1)   **Planning**: Deciding the objective and future course of action

(2)   **Organizing**: Assigning duties, grouping tasks, establishing authority and allocating resources

(3)   **Staffing:** Finding the right person for right position at right time

(4)   **Directing**: Issuing of instructions for performance of job

(5)   **Controlling**: Aim to ensure whether everything is done as per plan

Effectiveness: is concerned with doing the right task, completing activities and achieving goals on time

Efficiency: means doing the task correctly and with minimum cost.
Efficiency is increased when for the same benefit or output; fewer
resources are used and less cost are incurred.

Basis	Effectiveness	Efficiency
Meaning	It refers to completing the job on time, no matter whatever the cost	It refers to completing in the cost Efficient manner
Objective	To achieve end result on time	It conduct cost benefit analysis
Main consideration	Time	cost

Q1. Identify the management function:

(i)   Grouping various activities, assigning duties and establishing
authority relationship

(ii)   Recruitment, selection, training and development of employees

(iii)   Monitoring function

(iv)   Formulation of policies and strategies

(v)   Division of activities and creation of organizational structure

(vi)   Supervision and motivation of employees

(vii)   Finding the right person for right position

(viii) Comparison of actual performance with standards

(ix)   Management in action

(x)   Manpower planning

Q2. i) If a manager is able to achieve the target of production of 5000 units but at higher cost. Is he efficient or effective?

ii) Process of designing and maintaining an environment in which individual work together in groups efficiently and effectively to accomplish selected aims

iii) A company set the target production of 100 garments per month at the estimated cost of Rs. 200 per garment. Mohan a worker worked double shift and manufacture around 150 garments at a cost of Rs.250 per garment.

Ravi another worker focuses on cost and handles resources very carefully. So he manufactures 90 garments at a cost of Rs.190 per garment.

Third worker maintained the balance and achieve target of 100 garments at a cost of the Rs.200 per garment.

a) Identify the quality possessed by Mohan, Ravi and what they are lacking.

b) What quality is possessed by third worker?

c) Which worker is preferred by management?

iv) Successful organization does not achieve their goals by chance but by following a process. Name the process

v) Production manager tries to produce goods with minimum cost. Name the concept which is being focused on by management

vi) Process of working with and through others to effectively achieve organizational objectives by efficiently using its. Name the process.

vii) "Planning, organizing, staffing, directing and controlling" is the sequence of function in a process. Name it.

viii) Intangible force which creates productive relationships among resources of an organization.

ix) Mr. Rawat is an effective but inefficient manager. What does this means?

Ans –

1. I) organizing

ii) Staffing

iii) Controlling

iv) Planning

v) Organizing

vi) Directing

vii) Staffing

viii) Controlling

ix) Directing

x) Staffing

Q2.

    (i)   Effective

    (ii)   Management

    (iii)   (a) Mohan :Effective but inefficient, Ravi: efficient but ineffective

           (b) He is effective as well as efficient

(c) Third worker is preferred by management

(iv)   Management

(v)   Efficiency

(vi)   Management

(vii)   Management

(viii) Management

(ix)   Mr. Rawat is able to achieve his targets but at higher cost.

CHARACTERISTICS OR FEATURES OF MANAGEMENT

Terms to understand

(i)   **Goal oriented**: concerned with or focused on achieving a particular aim or result

(ii)   **Pervasive**: present or noticeable in every part of a thing or place

(iii) **Multi-dimensional**: anything with many different parts or aspects

(iv)   **Continuous**: without a pause or interruption

(v)   **Group activity**: activity conducted by an organized body of people

(vi)   **Dynamic**: Characterized by constant change

(vii) **Intangible**: unable to touch; not having physical presence

Characteristics Of management:(**My Charming Dad Is Giving Grand Party**)(**MCD PIGG**)

1.   **<u>Management is a goal oriented process:</u>** Management integrates the efforts of all members towards achieving certain organizational objectives (goals).

Management easily realizes the goals of the organization by fostering unitedness in the efforts of different employees.

Every organization exists to achieve some common goals. management aims at achieving such goals efficiently and effectively.

2.   **<u>Management is all pervasive</u>**: the activities in management are applicable to every type of   organization whether commercial or non-commercial, social, charitable, religious or political.

3.   **<u>Management is Multidimensional or multi-faceted</u>**: management is complex activity that has three main dimensions. These are:

(a)   **<u>Management of work</u>**: it is concerned with performance of task in an organization.

(b)   **<u>Management of People</u>**: managing people has two dimensions

(i)   It implies dealing with diverse needs of employees as individuals.

(ii)   It also implies dealing with individuals as a group of people.

(c)   **<u>Management of Operations</u>**: it Combines management of work as well as people to produce the goods. it involves deciding what is to be done and who is to do it.

4.   **<u>Management is a continuous Process</u>**: All the functions of management are performed by the managers on continuous basis. It is a never ending process. It is concerned with constantly identifying the problems and solving them by taking adequate steps. Management starts at the formation of the company and end when the company dissolves.

5.   **Management is a Dynamic Functions**: several constituents of environment namely social, economic and political continue to change. In order to overcome these changes successfully, management has to adopt itself to the changing environment by changing its goals and policies.

6.   **Management of group activity**: A single person cannot do different activities like purchase, sale, manufacturing, finance etc. But several people have to join hands together to perform them. Therefore we say that management is a group activity not an activity performed by a single person.

7.   **Management is an Intangible force**: Management cannot be seen, Its presence can be felt when targets are met, employees are happy and there is orderliness and coordination in the work environment.

Questions related to characteristics of management:

(1)   "Anything minus management is nothing". What do you mean by 'anything' and 'nothing' here? What does this statement signifies?

(2)   How management does realize the goals of the organization?

(3)   What are the two main issues before the management concerning its people?

(4)   Name the tool which helps use of human and non-human resources to fulfill the pre-determined goals?

(5)   "No goals in hand –no need of management" what does this statement signifies? Which characteristic of management it refers to?

(6)   What helps the management in achieving organizational goals?

(7)   Name the activity which starts at the formation of the company and ends when the company dissolves?

(8)   Highlight the characteristics of management:

i) In order to be successful, an organization must change its goal according to the need of the environment.

ii) planning, organizing, staffing, directing and controlling applied in organization such as school, clubs, restaurants, hospitals etc.

iii) The task of management is its make work towards achieving the organizational goals by making employees strengths effective and their weakness irrelevant.

iv) Bhuvan argues that management is required in all kinds of organization.

v) An organization is a collection of diverse individual with different needs.

vi) Domino's pizza's keep introducing new varieties of pizzas in its menu.

vii) Directors assigned task of implementing the plans and policies framed by the boards to all the departmental heads. Departmental appointed supervisors executives etc. So that the work can be assigned to worker as per the plans. Supervisors keep a check on workers as per plans.

viii) A petrol pump is needed to be as much as school.

ix) Why is management considered multifaceted concept?

x) Managers in India do same work as managers in U.S.A or Japan.

xi) A collection of diverse individuals with different needs but working towards fulfilling the common organizational goals.

xii) Management consists of an offering series of functions.

xiii) Management requires to build team work and coordination of individual effort in common direction.

xiv) An organization interacts with external environment and adopts itself to the changing environment.

ANSWERS

1. Anything refers to all types of activities such as business and non-business activities.

   Nothing refers to failure or loss

   This statement tells about the importance of management

2. Management easily realizes the goals of the organization by fostering unitedness in the efforts of different employees. The task of management is its make work towards achieving the organizational goals by making employees strengths effective and their weakness irrelevant.

3. (i)   It implies dealing with diverse needs of employees as individuals.

   (ii)   It also implies dealing with individuals as a group of people.

4. Management

5. This statement signifies that all the activities of manager are directed or focused on achieving a particular aim or result. It also means that if there are no goals to be achieved, manager need not have to perform any activity.

   Characteristic- management is a goal oriented process

6. Employees working in the organization

7. Management

8. (i) Management is a dynamic function

(ii) Management is all pervasive

(iii) Management is goal oriented process

(iv) Management is all pervasive

(v) Management is a group activity

(vi)Management is a dynamic function

(vii) Management is a Group Activity

(viii) Management is all pervasive

(ix) management is complex activity that has three main dimensions. These are:

(a)   **Management of work**: it is concerned with performance of task in an organization.

(b)   **Management of People**: managing people has two dimensions

(i)   It implies dealing with diverse needs of employees as individuals.

(ii)   It also implies dealing with individuals as a group of people.

(c)   **Management of Operations**: it Combines management of work as well as people to produce the goods. it involves deciding what is to be done and who is to do it.

(x) Management is all pervasive

(xi) Management is multidimensional- management of people

(xii) Management as a process

(xiii) Management is a group activity

(xiv) Management is a dynamic function

<u>Objectives Of management:</u>

1. **<u>Organizational Objectives</u>**: They are needed to achieve economic goals of the organizations. Three main organizational objectives are.

(i) **<u>Survival</u>**: possible only when organizations are able to earn enough revenue to cover its costs. By taking positive decisions with regard to different business activities management ensures that business survive for long.

(ii) **<u>Profits</u>**: An organization aims to earn adequate profits in order to face business hazards and successful running of the business activities. To achieve profits management must aim:

(a)   Getting maximum results with minimum efforts

(b) Increase the efficiency of factors of production.

(iii) **<u>Growth</u>**: management must exploit fully the growth potential of the business to survive in the long run.

2. **<u>Social Objectives</u>**: They are needed to achieve benefits of the society.

(i)   Supply of quality products at fair prices.

(ii)   Conducting business in lawful manner

(iii)   Environmental friendly method of production

(iv)   Giving employment opportunities to the disadvantaged section of the society

(v)   Providing basic amenities like schools and crèches to employees.

3. **<u>Personal Objectives</u>**: They relate to individuals needs of the employees like:

(i) **<u>Financial needs</u>** like competitive salary and other perks.

(ii) **<u>Social needs</u>** like peer recognition

(iii**<u>) High level needs</u>** like sufficient opportunities for personal development

Ques-1. Highlights the objective of management.
i) To meet the objectives of the firm, management of the anger. Ltd offers employment to physically challenged persons.
ii) Management of any organization strives to attain objectives of survival.
iii) Using ecofriendly method of production.
iv) Arranging yoga classes for its employees to improve their concentration level.
v) A barium ltd needs to add its project in the long run.
vi) Installing a special recycling plant to recycle the waste instead of dumping waste in ground.
vii) Providing employment opportunities to local resident.
viii) Started a school nearby for the children of their employees.
ix) Manager is very efficient and effective and makes sure all the employees and workers in his team perform the task on time with minimum cost. His main focus is on cost cutting so he never listens to the demand of workers for increasing wages. He even gives no opportunities to workers for promotions. As a result workers started becoming frustrated and disheartened all the time.
a) Which object of Management could not be achieved by manager?
x) Employment to physically challenged person.
xi) A business is running successfully for the last three years in Jaipur. Management has decided to focus on other states to sell their products.
xii) An achievement of which organizational objective result is "an increase in sales volumes, increase in numbers of employees, number of products and increase in capital investment".

Ques-2. What should an organization do to achieve the basic objective of survival?

Ques-3. "Survival, profit and growth are essential targets of any business".

Which objective of Management is referred here?

ANSWERS

Q1.

i.   Social objective

ii.   Economic objective

iii.   Social objective

iv.   Personal objectives

v.   Economic objective

vi.   Social objective

vii.   Social objective

viii.   Social objective

ix.   Personal objectives

x.   Social objectives

xi.   Economic objectives

xii.   Economic objectives

Q2. At least recover its cost. Survival is possible only when organizations are able to earn enough revenue to cover its costs. By taking positive decisions with regard to different business activities management ensures that business survive for long.

Q3. Economic objectives

<u>Importance of management:</u>

1**. <u>Management helps in achieving group goals</u>**: It brings the human and non-humans resources together and gives common directions to efforts of all individuals towards achieving the organizational goals.

2**. <u>Management Increases efficiency</u>**: through the optimum utilization of all the resources such as man, material, machine and money.

3. **<u>Management creates dynamic organization</u>**: Management helps people to adapt to environmental changes by convincing the employees that changes will benefits their future prospects.

4. **<u>Management helps in achieving personal objectives</u>**: Through motivation and leadership, management helps the individuals to achieve their personal goals while working towards organizations objectives.

5. **<u>Management helps development of society</u>**: While achieving the development of organization management also aims to develop society by giving due importance to social obligations.

6. **<u>Management create sound organization structure</u>**: It develops spirit of cooperative and mutual understanding and provides friendly environment in the organizations.

Ques-1. "Management is the life giving element in every business, without it the resources of production remains resources and shall never become production". Comment.
Ques-2. "Without effective Management, the resources will remain as resources and cannot be converted into productive utilities". Do

you agree? Give reason.

Ques-3. Success of an organization largely depends upon its Management Give reason to justify.

Ques-4. Highlight the importance of Management:

i) brings human and non-human resources together;

ii) gives a common direction to effort of all individuals towards achieving organizational goals.

iii) Reduce the cost.

iv) Increase productivity.

v) Help people adopt to change.

vi) Helps the individual to develop team spirit, cooperation and commitment to growing success.

vii) It gives due importance to social obligation.

viii) Helps to provide good quality products and service, creates employment opportunities, adopt new technology.

<u>ANSWERS</u>

1. Explain importance of management

2. Explain importance of management

3. Explain importance of management

4. (i) Management helps in achieving group goals

   (ii) Management helps in achieving group goals

   (iii) Management Increases efficiency

   (iv) Management Increases efficiency

   (v) Management creates dynamic organization

   (vi) Management create sound organization structure

   (vii) Management helps development of society

(viii) Management helps development of society

Nature Of management-Science, Art or Profession

Management as science:

1.   **Systematized body of knowledge**: Management satisfy this features as it also has a systematized body of knowledge built up by management practitioners over a considerable period of time like own theories, concepts and principles.

2.   **Principle based on Experimentations**: principles of management have evolved over a period of time based on repeated experiments and observations in different types of organization. Management came into existence because of continuous and encouraging labor of the theorists and various people concerned.

3.   **Universal validity**: management knowledge and principles of management are considered to be based on truth and they too can be applied anywhere and every situation but Management principal have to be modified according to a given situation as they deal with human behavior which is affected by culture, religion, beliefs etc. and also human behavior is highly unpredictable.

4.   **Cause and effect Relationship**: Outcomes of principal of management may vary in different situations. So it is difficult to predict the accurate outcome in management as in science.

Hence we conclude from above that management is not exact science rather it is inexact science.

Management as an Art:

1.   **Existence of theoretical knowledge**: there is lot of literature available in various areas of management like marketing, finance and

human resources which the manager has to specialize in.Thus this features is present as it involves use of theoretical knowledge like principal and techniques

2. **Personalized application**: A manager applies his acquired knowledge in a personalized and skillful manner in the light of the realities of a given situation. Every manager has his own unique way of managing things and peoples, although all managers learn same management theories and principals.

3. **Based on practice and creativity**: A good manager works through a combination of practice, creativity, imagination, initiative and innovation. A manager achieves perfection through long practice. Students of management also apply these principles differently depending on how creative they are.

Hence we conclude that management is an art as it satisfies all the characteristics.

III **Management as a profession**

1. **Well defined body of knowledge**: well defined principles based on variety of business situations- acquired in universities and colleges

2. **Restricted entry**: Management is open to all individuals who want to learn skills of management. No restrictions on anyone being designated as manager in business enterprise.

3. **Professional association**: It is not compulsory for a manager to be member of any management association like AIMA (All India Management Association)

4. **Ethitical code of conduct**: although there is certain code of conduct laid down by AIMA, there is not any compulsion for the managers to follow them.

5. **Service motive**: although management helps the organization to achieve its stated goal like social objectives but Management aims to accomplish organizational goals which are generally profit maximization.

-We conclude that management does not possess all the necessary feature of a profession.

Ques-1. A manager applies the various theories of management in his unique personalized way. What aspect of nature of management does their statement indicate?

Ques-2. Your father's wanted to do MBA before joining family business. What aspect of nature of management does their statement indicate

Ques-3. A manager uses his creativity and practice management principles under different situations to manage the business. The employees are happy and satisfied as he everyday rewards employees for their punctuality and efficiency. Identify the nature of management highlighted above.

Ques-4. Group of people believes that management is a systematic body of knowledge that explain certain general truth and it based on logical observation.

Identify and explain the nature of management discussed above.

Ques-5. There is no restriction in any one being appointed or designated as a manager of any business organization.

What aspect of management as a profession does this statement indicate?

Ans - It is a profession but act a full-fledged profession like medicine or law.

Ques-6. How is entry to profession restricted?

Ques-7. Management is based on personalized application of knowledge. Which nature of management is significant have?

Ques-8. "Management had its own theory and principles, vocabulary of terms and concepts". Which features of

science justified by management have?
Ques-9. Principles of management are not exact as principles of science and they have to be modified according to a given situation. Which feature is science is not applicable here.

ANSWERS

1. Management is an art

2. Management is a profession

3. Management is an art

4. Management is a science

5. Management is a profession

6. Only those who qualifies certain examination or acquires an educational degree are allowed to enter profession

7. Management is an art

8. Systematized body of knowledge

9. Universal validity and Cause and effect Relationship.

LEVELS OF MANAGEMENT

All the employees working in the organization can be divided into two categories-

(1) <u>Managerial members</u>- include CEO, departmental managers, supervisors etc. They are called managers because they manage some or the other person.

(2) <u>Non-managerial members</u>- include workers. They are the lowest level of chain in an organization, they do not have any sub-ordinates that is why they are cannot be called managers.

Levels of management

1. **Top level management**: Board of directors, chairman, president , CEO, COO, general manager, managing director etc.

Functions:

1. **Determine the objectives** of organization

2. **Framing of plans and policies** for realization of objectives

3. **Analyze the business environment.**

4. **Setting up an organizational frame work.**

5. **Assemble the resources** like raw material, fixed assets etc.

6. **Approving budgets** prepared by different managers.

7. **Controlling the work performance** to get the desired results.

2. **Middle level management**: Purchase manager, production manager, finance manager, plant superintendent, divisional heads, departmental heads, deputy departmental heads, operation managers etc.

Functions

1. **Interpret the policies** framed by top management

2. **Selecting suitable supervisory personnel**.

3. **Assign duties and responsibilities** to lower management

4. **Motivate personnel** to achieve desired objectives.

5. **preparing organizational set up**: prepare outline of his respective departments according with objectives of organization.

6. **Issuing instructions:** Direct their subordinates about what to do and how they have to do it.

7. **Creating cooperation** between different departments.

3. **Operational or supervisory level or lower level management**: Supervisor, superintendent, foreman, section officer etc.

Functions:

1. Issues orders and instructions.

2. Prepare plan for activities.

3. Assign and assist in work.

4. **Represents workers grievances.** to middle level managers.

5. **ensuring proper working environment:** by arranging water, electricity, ventilation, cleanliness etc.

6. **Inviting suggestions** from subordinates to improve the quality of work.

Ques-1. Identify the level of management:
i) Overseeing the activities of workers.

ii) Taking key decisions.
iii) Purchase manager, CEO, superintendent, foreman, and manager. iv) Selection of employees.
v) Introducing new products.
vi) Design a suitable advertisement; companion to sell a new products.
vii) Framing the capital structure of the company.
viii) Preparing performance report of employees. ix) Hiring casual

labor.
x) Responsible for welfare and survival organization.
xi) A company wants to modernize its products. What functions or decisions should be taken by each level to carry on this task?

xii) Arun is responsible for welfare of whole organization. He has to develop long term objectives, policies and review the work of different needs at different level.
xiii) Arun is responsible for the working of department he is heading, formulate that term departmental objectives in accordance with organizational objectives. xiv) Archana is in direct contact with workforce consists of work and providing good working conditions to worker's.
xv) Liasion with outside work.
xvi) Miss Archana is associated with sugar Ltd. She told you that her workers have good relations with her. At what level of management is the?
xvii) The authority responsibility relationship that binds individuals as supervisors and subordinated in organization, gives rise it's what?
xviii) They transmit orders, decisions and guidance down wards, they also deals with problems and solutions.

ANSWERS

(I)   Operational level management

(II)   Top level

(III)   middle level

(IV)   middle level

(V)   top level

(VI)   middle level

(VII) top level

(VIII) middle level

(IX)   lower level

(X)   top level

(XI)   Top level management:

(i) they must plan the technique of modernisation

(ii) they must organise and assemble necessary resources

(iii) they must coordinate the efforts of all the departments towards modernisation

Middle level management:

(i) they must implement the plans made by top level in their respective departments

(ii) they must interpret the plans to their subordinates

(iii) they must recruit and select necessary employees to carry on the task.

(iv) they must motivate the personnel to work towards   accomplishment of task

Lower/supervisory level:

(i) they must assign the task to work force

(ii) they must supervise that the task is carried on in the right direction

(iii) they must maintain the quality of work and reduce the wastage

(iv) they must make efforts to improve the loyalty of workers

(XII) Top level

(XIII) Middle level

(XIV) lower level

(XV) top level

(XVI) Lower level

(XVII)   Level of management

(XVIII)   Middle level

<u>CO-ORDINATION</u>

-       The process by which a manager synchronizes the activities of different departments is known as coordination.

-       It is the force that binds all other functions of management

-       It is a common thread that runs through all the activities such as purchase, sales and finance to ensure continuity in the working of the organization.

- it is implicit and inherent in all the functions of the organization.

Q. Is co-ordination a separate function of management? Explain.

No, rather Co-ordination is an Essence of management because of the following two reasons:

1. **<u>Co-ordination is needed in all management functions</u>**:

(a) **Planning:**

- Between overall plan of organization and departmental plans.

- Draft plans keeping in mind activities already being performed by various departments

(b) **Organizing**:

- Between resources and activities to be performed.

- Authority, responsibility & accountability

- Different departments

- Different people working in the same department

(c) **Staffing**:

- Between efficiency of workers and compensation.

- Skills of the person and job assigned to him

(d) **Directing:**

- Between superiors and subordinates.

- Order, instructions, guidelines and suggestions provided

(e) **Controlling**:

- Between standards and actual performance.

- Harmonization objectives, available resources and human efforts involved

2. Co-ordination is needed at all levels:

(a)   **Top level**:

- to integrate all the activities of organization for accomplishment of goals.

- Lead the efforts of all individuals in one common direction

(b)   **Middle level:**

- to integrate efforts of different sections and sub-sections.

(c)   **Lower level**:

- in the activities of worker to ensure that work proceeds as per plans.

<u>Characteristics of co-ordination</u>

1.   <u>**Co-ordination integrates group efforts:**</u>

- coordination is an orderly arrangement of group efforts and not an individual effort.

- It gives common focus to group efforts to ensure that performance is as it was planned and schedule.

- Integration of all individual efforts from different backgrounds & with different style of work in one common direction

2.   <u>**Co-ordination ensures unity of action**</u>:

- it acts as a binding force between departments and ensures that all efforts are focused towards achieving organizational goals.

- Unify activities of different groups towards one goal

3. **<u>Co-ordination is a continuous process</u>**:

- coordination is a never ending process as its needs is felt at each and every step in the organization. It begins at the planning stage and continues till controlling.

- Required so as to maintain a balance between various activities undertaken

4. **<u>Co-ordination is all pervasive functions</u>**:

- coordination is needed in all departments and at all levels due to interdependent nature of activities of various departments

- it integrates the efforts of different departments and different levels

5. **<u>Co-ordination is a deliberate function</u>**:

- Coordination is never established by itself but it is a deliberate or conscious effort of managers.

- Co-ordination leads to successful accomplishment of task & avoid confusion and chaos

6. **<u>Coordination is the responsibility of all managers</u>**:

(a) **Top level**: need to coordinate with their subordinates to ensure that overall policies for the organization are duly carried out.

(b) **<u>Middle level</u>**: to integrate efforts of different sections and sub-sections. To coordinate with both the top level and first line managers.

(c)   **<u>Lower level</u>**: in the activities of worker to ensure that work proceeds as per plans.

<u>Importance of coordination</u>(FISS):It integrates the efforts of individuals, departments and specialists

Primary reason for coordination is that departments and individuals in the organization are interdependent.

(i) **<u>Growth in size</u>**: number of employees increases as organization grows in size. Individuals differ in their habitsof work, background, approach to the situations and relationship with others.

- coordination helps to harmonize individual objectives with organizational objectives as the size of organization increases, number of employees also rises.

- Greater the number of people involved, more the difficulties in achieving the objectives due to differences in interest, working style, objectives, understanding and tolerance

- Coordination ensures a proper environment is available for all so as each one can fully contribute to his/her maximum towards achievement of organizational goals

(ii) **<u>Functional differentiation</u>** (departments): all the departments have their own objectives, policies and their own style of working . conflicts arises in the organization because each unit/department is performing activities in isolation from others . Barriers between departments are becoming more rigid. The process of linking the activities of various departments is accomplished by coordination

- Coordination helps to synchronize activities of various departments so that they proceed together in a single direction instead of working as independent units

- Organization consists of different interrelated and interlinked departments sections and divisions

- Need to bring together the activities of different departments, sections and divisions towards one common organizational goals for which coordination is required

(iii) **<u>Specialization</u>**: specialization arises out of the complexities of modern technology and the diversity of task to be performed. Specialist usually think that they are only qualified to evaluate, judge and decide according to their professional criteria. They do not take advice or suggestions from others in the matter pertaining to their area of specialization. This often leads to conflicts amongst different specialists and others in the organization

- Coordination helps to reconcile the differences in approach, interest or opinion of specialist.

- Division of main activities into various sub activities & allotment of task based upon areas of expertise to different individuals

- Every person performs the task to the best of his/her potential without considering total work to be done

- Coordination ensures accomplishment of overall goals and taking benefit of specialization

(iv) **<u>interdependence of different processes</u>**: all the units or departments are mutually inter-dependent that calls for coordination amongst all

Answer the following questions:

i) Binds all the functions of management?

Ans- Co-ordination

ii)   Success of dubbawala of Mumbai is an example of which aspect of management.

Co-ordination

iii)   Process by which manager synchronizes the activities of different department .

Co-ordination

iv)   ABC Ltd is facing a lot of problems these days. The company profit margin is declining day by day. The production manager is blaming marketing management whereas marketing is blaming production departments for not maintaining the quality. Finance department is blaming both. What quality of manager do you think in lacking? Explain it brief.

Co-ordination is lacking

v)   In an organization sales department wants to increase sales by 20% so sales department plans to offer extra discounts to customers. Finance department raised objection on it as they say it will result in loss of revenue and company may face liquidity problems.

(a)   Name the importance of coordination referred here.

    Functional differentiation

(b) State other two importance.

    (i)   Growth in size

    (ii)   Specialization:

vi)   Requires team work and integrations of efforts of all individual departments and specialists.

Importance of Co-ordination- Growth in size

vii)   Manager needs to reconcile differences in approach, timing, efforts and interest.

Importance of Co-ordination- specialization

viii)   Need to harmonize individual goals and organizational goals.

Importance of Co-ordination- functional differentiation

Ques-2. Identify which concept of management is used in following case:

a) When sales manager makes a plan to set sales target, he consult the same with production and finance manager.

Ans- Coordination in planning.

b) Production manager divides the work in such as manner as when one finishes the task; the other begins to work new.

Ans- Coordination in organizing.

<u>OBJECTIVE TYPE QUESTIONS</u>

<u>Objective Type Questions 1.1</u>

1. Complete the Sentence:
   Management is concerned with the efficient use of resources, because ……….

2. "High efficiency is associated with high effectiveness."

3. "Effectiveness means doing the task correctly and with minimum cost."

4. "Planning is the function of determining in advance what is to be done and who is to do it.

5. "Planning cannot prevent problems."

6. ………………….function of management decides who will do a particular task, where it will be done, and when it will be done.

7. Match the following function of management:

(i) Setting goals in advance and developing a way of achieving them effectively and efficiently	(a) Planning
(ii) Establishing an atmosphere that encourages employees to do their best.	(b) Organising
(iii) Determining what activities and resources are required	(c) Staffing
(iv) Recruitment selection, placement and training of personnel	(d) Directing
(v) Determining what activities and outputs are critical to success	(e) Controlling

8. Name the concept of management which involves the grouping of the required tasks into manageable work units and establishment of authority and reporting relationships within the organizational hierarchy.

9. ……………………………. function of management is also known as the human resource function.

10. One of the very important aspects of management is to make sure that the right people with the right qualification are available at the right places and times to accomplish the goals of the organization. Identify the aspect of management.

11. …………………….. is the management function of monitoring organizational performance towards the attainment of organizational goals.

12. ……………………………. is the function of management examines the activities and resources required to implement the plan.

13. "McDonalds, the fast food giant made major changes in its menu to be able to survive. State the characteristic of management highlighted in the above statement.

Q14. Match the following:

i. leading, influencing and motivating employees to perform the tasks assigned to them	a. Organizing
ii. Assigning dues grouping tasks, establishing authority and allocating resources required to Carry out a specific plan	b. Staffing
iii. Recruitment and selection of the personnel	c. directing

15 Which function of management is concerned with finding the right people for the right job?

16 In order to be successful an organization must change its goals according to the needs of the environment Which characteristic of management is highlighted in the statement?

17 Successful organizations do not achieve their goals by chance but by following a deliberate process". Identify the process highlighted here.

18 Which function of management relates to assigning duties, grouping tasks, establishing authority and allocating resources required to carry out a specific plan?

19 Match the complete column :

Matching outcomes with targets	(a) Planning
Objectives	(b) Organizing
Resources for implementation	(c) Directing
Recruitment and training	(d) Staffing`
Supervision and motivation	(e) Controlling

20 A production manager was able to produce the desired output with minimum cost but not within the required time. In this case the manager was:

   a)   Effective only
   b)   Efficient only
   c)   Both effective and efficient
   d)   Neither effective nor efficient

21 Name the process of working with and through others to effectively achieve organizational objectives by efficiently using Limited resources in the changing environment.

22 Suhasini the General Manager of Fabmart, perform the managerial functions of planning, organising, staffing directing and controlling as an ongoing process. Which management feature is highlighted by this?

23 Why is management considered a multi-faceted concept?

<u>**Objective type Question 1.2**</u>

   1.   Which of the following is not an indicator of growth of an organisation?
        (a) Increase in number of employees
        (b) Increase in number of products

(c) increase in capital investment

(d) None of the above

2. The following is not an objective of management:

   (a) earning profits

   (b) growth of the organization

   (c) providing employment

   (d) policy making

3. To meet the objectives of the firm, the Asian Paints contributed large amount of funds to enable farmers to use local resources effectively. Identify the management objective it tried to achieve.

4. Radhika Ltd. uses environment-friendly methods of production. Identify the objective it is trying to achieve.

5. In this first year of operation, the revenues generated by Max Industries from sale of its products are just sufficient to cover the cost of production. Which organizational objective is met in the given case?

6. Raheja Ltd. is diversifying its product lines. What organizational objective it is trying to achieve?

7. To meet the objectives of the firm, the management of Bhavya Ltd. offers employment to physically challenged persons. Identify the organizational objective it is trying to achieve.

8. The main objective of any organization should be to utilize human and material resources to the maximum possible advantage, ie to fulfill the economic objectives of a business. Enumerate the economic objectives of a business.

9. Through ………….. management helps individuals to develop team spirit, cooperation and commitment to group success.

10. The authority-responsibility relationship binds individuals as superiors and subordinates and gives rise to different …………………… in an organization.

11. The main task of the middle level managers is …………………….

12. ……………………… comprises the lower level in the hierarchy of the organization.

13. Supervisory level management plays a very important role of the organization since ………..

14. Name the level of management: (i) overseeing the efforts of the workforce (ii) formulating organizational goals

15. Foremen and Supervisors comprise ………………..

   (a) Top level of management (b) Middle level of management (c) Operational management (d) None of these

16. Ritu is the manager of the northern division of a large corporate house. At what level of management does she work in the organization? What is her main task?

17. Your grandfather is working in an MNC as chief operating officer. At which level of management he is working.

18. At which level of management are the managers responsible for maintaining the quality of output and the safety standards?

19. Name the level of management at which the managers are responsible for implementing and controlling the plans and strategies of the organization.

20. At which level of management the managers are responsible for the welfare and survival of the organization?

21. Sarthak Jain is responsible for framing plans and policies of Neel Madhav Ltd. At which managerial level, he is working?

22. Match the following activities with their respective levels of management:

(i) Introducing a new product line and deciding the capital structure of the company	(a) Top management
(ii) Recruitment of casual labourers.	(b) Middle management
(iii) Devise a suitable advertising campaign to sell a new product/ service a company is launching.	(c) Supervisory or Operational management

23. Dheeraj is working as 'Operations Manager' in Tifco Ltd. Name the managerial level at which he is working.

24. Name the level of management which is a team consisting of managers from different functional levels, heading finance marketing, etc, for example, chief finance officer, vice president (marketing).

Objective Type Questions 1.3

1. Management is the systematized body of knowledge that explains certain general truths" Identify the nature of the management highlighted in the statement
2. Management is skillful and personal application of existing knowledge to achieve desired results. Identify the nature of management highlighted in the statement
3. Which of the following statement best explains the "Management is an Art"?
   a) Two managers deal with the same problem differently. (b) Management has drawn its knowledge from other disciplines also. c) No formal qualification is required for the appointment as a manager in a company d) Outcomes of managerial actions cannot be predicted accurately.
4. Management is
   a) an art
   b) a science
   c) both art and science
   d) neither art nor science

5. Which of the following is not a characteristic of a profession?

(a) Service motive

b) Restricted entry

c)Based on practice and creativity

d)Is Well-defined body of knowledge.

6. in today's scenario, organizations look for individuals with specific qualifications and experience to manage them. It has also been observe that there has been an increase in the corporate form of business and increasing emphasis on managed business concerns. What does the above statement imply?

<u>**Objective Type Questions 1.4**</u>

1. The process of linking the activities of various departments is accomplished by …………………
2. Coordination is a one-time function   (True/False)
3. …………………involves synchronization of the different actions or efforts of the various units of an organization.
4. in the absence of …………………there is overlapping and chaos instead of harmony and integration of activities.
5. Coordination is the function of the top management   (True/False)
6. For organizational efficiency, it is important to harmonize individual goals and organizational goals through ……………………
7. Identify and state the force that binds all the other functions of management
8. The process by which a manager synchronizes the activities of different departments is known as …………………………….
9. Which of the following is not a function of management?
    (a) Planning
    (b) Staffing
    (c) Coordination
    (d)) Controlling
10. Coordination is
    (a) a function of management
    (b) Cooperation
    (c) an objective of management
    (d) None of the above
11. it is the force which binds all other functions of management. It is the common thread that runs through all activities such as purchase, production, sales and finance to ensure continuity in the working of the organization. Identify it
12. Name the process which provides the requisite amount, quality, timing and sequence of efforts and ensures that planned objectives are achieved with a minimum of conflict.
13. "Coordination is needed at all levels of management. "State the characteristic of coordination highlighted in the statement

<u>Objective type questions 1.5</u>

Fill In the Blanks:- (Based on remembrance)

1. The welfare and survival of an organization are the main functions performed by ……… level of management.

2. The overall organization goals and strategies of organization are formulated by ……….. level of management.

3. Divisional heads, department heads belongs to ……….. level of management

4. The operational level managers are also termed as   ………………

5. Lower level of management comprises of …………. and ………………..

6. Interpretation of the policies are done by ………… level of management.

7. Co-operation with various departments for smooth functioning of organization is done by ……… level of management.

8. Quality of output and safety standards are being maintained by …………. level of management

9. Co-ordination is an ………… of management

10. Co-ordination act as a ……………force between various departments to ensure unity of action.

11. Efficiency means doing the task correctly and with ……….. cost.

12. The Multidimensional characteristics of management links work, people and …………….

13. Management requires team work and coordination of individual effort in common …………..

14. Management is an ……… force that cannot be seen but its presence can be felt.

15. Management is a ………….. function to have adapt itself to the changing environment.

16. In order to survive an organization must earn enough revenues to cover ……..

17. Science principles are based on ……….. and …………..relationship.

18. Scientific principles are developed through ………………. and …………………..

19. Scientific principles have ……….. validity and application.

20. All professions are based on …………….. of knowledge

21. Management is …………….. as it includes management of work, people and operations.

22. Management is the process of getting things done with the aim of achieving goals ………….. and ………………….

23. Coordination is called the …………. of management.

24. …………………….level of management passes on the instructions of management to the workers.

25. The policies framed by the top management is …………….. by middle level of management.

26. Priya is using environmental friendly methods of production.She is trying to achieve …………………..objective of management.

27. Organisational objectives of management are …………I and ……….

28. Top level of management is responsible for ………………..and …………..of the organization.

29. Management increases …………….. by reducing costs and increasing productivity.

30. Management is a ……….. function as it adapts itself according to the changing environment.

True or False:- (Based on understanding and remembrance)

1. The basic objective of any profession is to earn money.

2. The top level of management are responsible for welfare and survival of organization.

3. Middle level of management implement the policies framed by top level of management.

4. Co-ordination is a separate function of management.

5. The main objective of any profession is to serve the society as a whole.

6. The top level of management are not responsible for all the activity of business and its impact on society.

7. Middle level of management motivate their team to achieve desired goals.

8. Co-operation in absence of co-ordination leads to waste of efforts.

9. Co-ordination without Co-operation may lead to dissatisfaction among employees.

10. Specialization arises out of complexities of modern technology and diversity of task to be performed.

11. Art does not involve the creative practice of existing theoretical knowledge.

12. Management is not a multidimensional activity.

13. Efficiency means doing the task correctly and with maximum cost.

14. For management it is necessary to be efficient rather than effective.

15. Management is a multidimensional activity.

16. The existence of management can be seen it cannot be felt.

17. The basic objective of any business is survival.

18. Management does not require team work and co-ordination of individual efforts in a common direction.

19. Through motivation and leadership management helps the individual to develop team spirit.

20. Management resist the people to adapt the changes in competitive world.

21. Scientific management principles are universally applicable.

22. Management principles are derived after observations and experimentations under controlled condition.

23. Coordination is not a separate function of management.

24. Management does not help in achieving personal objectives.

25. There are 3 levels of management in the hierarchy of an organization.

26. Middle level of management is the link between top and supervisory level of management.

27. Supervisory level managers are also known as divisional heads.

28. Coordination is the separate function of management.

29. Coordination involves synchronization of the different actions of the various units of the organization

30. Management is a full fledged profession like legal, accounting and medical profession.

31. Management is a science as well as an art

32. Coordination is the force that binds all the other functions of management.

33. Cooperation in the absence of coordination may lead to wasted effort

34. Coordination without cooperation may lead to dissatisfaction among employees.

Multiple choice question

1. Profit is essential for covering cost and risk of the business.Which management objective is discussed here?

a) Social objective

b) Organistional objective

c) Personal objective

d) Individual objective

2. Ankita is engaged in manufacturing chocolates and biscuits by using environmental friendly methods of production. Which management objective is used here?

a) Individual objective

b) Organisational objective

c) Social objective

d) Economic objective

3. Sachin the director of Apex ltd.is engaged in manufacturing furniture. He decided to keep one-third seats reserved for specially disadvantaged section of society. Which objective of management is discussed here?

a) Individual objective

b) Social objective

c) Organisational objective

d) Personal objective

4. When an organization is concerned about personal growth and development of employees which management objective is highlighted?

a) Organisational objective

b) Personal objective

c) Social objective

d) Growth objective

5. Identify the feature of management as a science when the principles are based on cause and effect relationship.

a) Based on practice and creativity

b) Universal validity

c) Systematised body of knowledge

d) Based on existence of theoretical knowledge

6. In order to enter into profession one has to acquire an educational degree by clearing specified examination conducted by registered institutes. Which feature of profession is being revealed?

a) Restricted entry

b) Ethical code of conduct

c) Professional association

d) Well defined body of knowledge

7. Which level of management is responsible for the welfare and survival of organization?

a) Middle level

b) Supervisory level

c) Operational level

d) Top level

8. Which level of management is concerned to develop cooperation with other departments for smooth functioning of organisation?

a) Top level

b) Supervisory level

c) Middle level

d) Operational level

9."It involves leading, influencing and motivating the employees to perform the assigned task", highlighted one of the function of management. Identify

a) Staffing

b) Planning

c) Directing

d) Controlling

10. Highlight the feature of management depicted by the image given here

a) Group activity   T- Together   E-Everyone
A-Achieves   M-More

b) Goal oriented

c) Pervasive

d) Dynamic

11. To exploit fully the growth potential of the organization management is talking about which objective?

a) Social objective

b) Personal objective

c) Organisational objective

d) Economic objective

12. In order to survive an organization must earn enough revenue to cover cost. Which management objective is highlighted?

a) Organistional objective

b) Growth objective

c) Social objective

d) Individual objective

13. Radhika is engaged in manufacturing earthen coolers by using environmental friendly methods of productions. Which management objective is discussed?

a) Social objective

b) Organisational objective

c) Individual objective

d) Economic objective

14. An organization is providing basic amenities like schools and crèches to employees. Which management objective is highlighted?

a) Organisational objective

b) Personal objective

c) Individual objective

d) Social objective

15. The style of singing of Arijit Singh and Honey Singh are to each other, however they acquired same knowledge of ragas.Identify the feature of art discussed above.

a) Based on practice and creativity

b) Universal validity

c) Existence of theoretical knowledge

d) Personalised application

16. In order to become a lawyer one has to register himself as a member of Bar Council of India. Which feature of profession is being revealed?

a) Ethical code of conduct

b) Restricted entry

c) Service motive

d) Professional association

17. Which level of management formulates overall organizational goals and strategies for their achievement?

a) Middle level

b) Operational level

c) Top level

d) Supervisory level

18. Which level of management is responsible to ensure their department has the necessary personnel?

a) Supervisory level

b) Middle level

c) Operational level

d) Top level

19. "Deciding in advance what is to be done and who is to do it" highlighted one of the functions of management. Identify it.

a) Organising

b) Planning

c) Directing

d) Controlling

20. It is not a separate fuction of management but its very essence.Identify it.

a) Cooperation

b) Efficiency

c) Coordination

d) Effectiveness

21.The process of getting things done through others is called

a)Effectively c)Efficiency

b)Management d)Planning

22.The force that binds all the other functions of management is called

a)Controlling c)Cooperation

b)Coordination d)Planning

23."Determining in advance what is to be done in future".Which function of management is highlighted in the above statement?

a)Staffing c)Planning

b)Directing d)Controlling

24."Management cannot be seen but its presence can be felt".Which characteristic of management is highlighted in the above statement?

a)Group activity c)Dynamic function

b)Intangible force d)Continuous process

25."Management has to adapt itself according to the changing environment".Which characteristic of management is highlighted in the above statement?

a)Continuous process c)Group activity

b)Dynamic function d)Goal oriented

26.Ram is working as a superintendent in a factory.State the level of management at which he is working?

a)Top level c)Supervisory level

b)Middle level d)Administrative level

27. Vipin is working as a marketing manager in Abc ltc.State the level of management at which he is working?

a)Top level c)Supervisory level

b)Middle level d)Operational level

28.Management consists of 3 dimensions-management of work,people and operations.Which characteristic of management is being highlighted here?

a)Goal oriented c)Multi dimensional

b)Dynamic d)Pervasive

29.An organization is a group of different individuals who work together with team spirit and coordination to achieve the goals of the organization.Which characteristic of management is being highlighted in the above statement?

a)Goal oriented c)Pervasive function

b)Group activity d)Continuous process

30.This concept provides the requisite amount,quality ,timing and sequence of efforts which ensures that planned objectives are achieved with a minimum of conflict.Identify the concept identified in the above stated line.

a)Cooperation c)Coordination

b)Management d)Planning

Match the columns

1. identifying the levels of management :

2) They interact with the actual workforce

3) Responsible for all the activities of business and its impact on society

2. identifying the management functions:

1) It involves monitoring organization performance towards attainment of organizational goals

2) Deciding in advance what to do and how to do

3. identify the importance of coordination:

a) When all departments have their own objectives, policies and their own style of working

b) When organization is performing on large scale and more people are employed

c) When more complexities of modern technology and diversity of tasks is to be performed

4. importance of management:

a) The task of the mangers is to reduce the cost and to increase the productivity

b) Job of the manager is to give common direction to individual efforts

c) Organization have to work in an environment which is constantly changing

5. nature of management:

1) Principles are based on observation and experimentation

2) Principles are based on practice and creativity

6. Match the columns on the basis of objectives of management

a) Essential for covering cost and risks of the business

b) A business needs to add to its prospects in the long run

c) An organization must have enough revenues to cover cost

7. identify the importance of coordination:

(a) When all departments have their own objectives, policies and their own style of working

(b) When organization is performing on large scale and more people are employed

(c) When more complexities of modern technology and diversity of tasks is to be performed

8. nature of management:

a) Professional association

b) Personalized application

c) Systematized body of knowledge

d) Existence of theoretical knowledge

9. importance of management:

a) The task of the mangers is to reduce the cost and to increase the productivity

b) Job of the manager is to give common direction to individual efforts

c) Helps to provide quality production and creates employment opportunities

10. objectives of management:

a. Essential for covering cost and risks of the business

b. An organization must have enough revenues to cover cost

c. A business needs to add to its prospects in the long run

11. identifying the levels of management :

1) Managers are responsible for the welfare and survival of organization

2) They ensure that the departments have necessary personnel

12. identifying the management functions:

1) It bridges the gap between where we are and where we want to be

2) Process of assigning the duties, grouping tasks, establishing authority and allocating resources

13. identify the features of coordination:

a) Coordination is the function performed by every manager

b) It begins at planning stage and continues till planning

c) Manager has to coordinate the efforts of different people in cautious manner

14.identify the importance of coordination:

a) When all departments have their own objectives, policies and their own style of working

b) When organization is performing on large scale and more people are employed

c) When more complexities of modern technology and diversity of tasks is to be performed

15. nature of management:

1) Its principles have universal validity and applicability

2) There is restrictions through an examination for acquiring educational degree

Q16. importance of management:

1) Job of the manager is to give common direction to individual efforts

2) The task of the mangers is to reduce the cost and to increase the productivit

17. objectives of management

a) An organization must have enough revenues to cover cost

b) Essential for covering cost and risks of the business

c) A business needs to add to its prospects in the long run

18. features of management:

1) The presence of management cannot be seen but it can be felt the way the organization functions

2) For success an organization must change itself according to the need of an environment

19. nature of management as an art and science

a) Systematized body of knowledge

b) Ethical code of conduct

c) Personalized application

d) Professional association

20. identifying the functions of management:

1) It is the process of finding the right person for the right job

2) It involves leading, influencing and motivating the employees to perform the assigned task

21 characteristics of management.

 1) Management unites individual effort in a

common direction.

2) Management is required in all types of org.

3) Management cannot be seen but its presence can be felt.

22. meaning.

1) Process by which a manager synchronises the activities of different departments.

 2) It is deciding in advance what is to be done in future.

3) Process of getting things done effectively and efficiently.

23. the levels of management

a) Top level of management

 ii) Chief financial officer

iii) Marketing Manager

iv)Superintendent

24. functions of management with the role it performs.

 i) Establishing authority responsibility relationship.

 ii) Finding the right people for the right job.

iii) Determining in advance what is to be done in future.

iv) Monitoring organizational performance.

25. objectives of management.

 i) Satisfying financial, social and higher level needs of employee

 ii) Creating economic value for the society

iii) Survival, profit and growth

iv)Creating employment opportunities

26. levels of management.

 i) Interpret the policies framed by top management.

 ii) Maintains quality of output and reduce wastage of resources.

iii) Analyse the business environment and its implications for the survival of the firm iv)Oversee the work of workers

27. levels of management.

i) They interact with the actual workforce and pass on the instructions of middle level management to the workers.

ii) They assign necessary duties and responsibilities to the personnel and motivate them to achieve the objectives.

iii) They are responsible for all activities of the business and for its impact on society.

iv)they see to it that their department has necessary personnel

28. features of coordination.

A) Coordination is the responsibility of all the managers

B) A manager has to coordinate the efforts of different people in a conscious manner.

C) Coordination unifies diverse Interests into purposeful work activity

29. characteristics of management.

i) Management is the process of continuous but separate functions of

ii) Management has to adapt itself acc to the changing environment.

iii) Manangement has 3 dimensions-mgt of work,people and operations

iv)Management is series of ongoing functions

30. features of coordination

i) Coordination is not a one time function

ii) Coordination is the function of every manager in the organization.

iii)Coordination is required at all levels of Management.

iv)Coordination act as a binding force and ensures that all the action is aimed at achieving the goals of the organization.

Multiple Choice Questions-I

1. The process of creating an internal environment, where individual work effectively

and efficiently for achievement of goal is known as

(a) Coordination (b) Delegation

(c) Management (d) Planning

2. When a worker achieves target production of 100 unit at a higher cost, he is

(a) Efficient (b) Effective

(c) Both Effective and Efficient (d) None of the above

3. Management is a process because

(a) It involves series of steps (b) It leads to systematic working

(c) It involves one single activity (d) None of the above

4. Management is always denoted by 'We' and not by 'I' because

(a) It is a process (b) It is continuous

(c) It is a group activity (d) It is intangible

5. Management works with the following objectives

(a) Objective of profit maximisation

(b) Objective of sales maximisation

(c) Objective of becoming market leader

(d) Multiple objective

6. A good manager focuses on

(a) Prosperity of management

(b) Prosperity of employees

(c) Prosperity of both management and employees

(d) None of the above

7. Managers apply management principles by using creativity. This is related to

(a) Management as Science

(b) Management as an Art

(c) Management as both Science and Art

(d) Management as a profession

8. Liaison with the outside world is the function of

(a) Top Level (b) Supervisory Level

(c) Middle Level (d) All of the above

9. Providing good working conditions and ensuring quality work is the function of

(a) Top Level (b) Middle Level .

(c) Supervisory Level (d) All of the above

10. As Top Level is responsible for the welfare and operations of whole organisation,

Middle Level is responsible for the welfare and operations of

(a) Workers (b) Department

(c) Both (a) and (b) (d) None of the above

11. Coordination is

(a) A function of management (b) An essence of management

(c) Part of Management (d) None of the above

12. Which function of management ensures work accomplishment as per plan?

(a) Planning (b) Directing

(c) Controlling (d) Organising

13. The process by which a manager integrates and synchronises the activities of

different department is called

(a) Management (b) Controlling

(c) Planning (d) Coordination

14. Coordination is more important in an organisation-

(a) Performing or dealing with single function

(b) Performing or dealing with multiple functions

(c) Performing or dealing with manufacturing goods

(d) All of the above

15. All the businessmen prefer their children to do MBA and then join business. This is

related to

(a) Management as Science (b) Management as an Art

(c) Management as a profession (d) Management as both Science and Art

FILL IN THE BLANKS

1. The management of an organisation does not achieve its objective by chance, but it

is done by following a process called ___________________.

2. The function of management, which creates various departments is called

___________________.

4 Business Studies

3. The primary or first function of every manager is

___________________.

4. Division/Department head belongs to ___________________ Level of management.

5. Managers must update and modify its objectives from time to time is indicated in

_________________________ feature of management.

6. Management has _________________________ objectives.

7. Completing the task with minimum cost and optimum utilisation of resources is

called _________________________.

8. Completing the task on time or achievement of target is called

_________________________.

9. Increase in number of branches, number of products indicate that management is

achieving _________________________ objective.

10. Coordination does not come by chance but is a _________________________ process.

TRUE OR FALSE

1. Management is a single activity.

2. Management is used only in Business Organisations.

3. Management work with the single objective of Profit Maximisation.

4. Management is a group activity.

5. Coordination is a function of management.

Multiple Choice Questions-II

1. How does a manager want to achieve his objectives?

(a) Efficiently (b) Effectively

(c) Efficiently and effectively (d) None of the above

2. A manager obtains the required capital at 12% interest while the prevailing

rate of interest happens to be 10%. How would you describe such a manager?

(a) Efficient (b) Effective

(c) Efficient and Effective (d) Inefficient

3. What type of power management is?

(a) Visible (b) Invisible

(c) Separate (d) Collective

4. By evaluating results what does management try to find out and then takes

corrective action.

(a) Profit (b) Loss

(c) Deviations (d) None of these

5. In the context of business what does research refer to?

(a) Finding out new products

(b) Finding out new markets

(c) Finding out new methods of distribution

(d) All the above

6. What happens when the management of an organisation gets weakened?

(a) Organisation progresses (b) Production increases

(c) Profit increases (d) Organisation faces heavy loss

7. Which one of the following sequence of process of management is correct:

(a) Planning, Controlling, Organising, Staffing

(b) Staffing, Planning, Organising, Controlling

(c) Planning, Organising, Staffing, Controlling

(d) Organising, Planning, Staffing, Controlling

8. Management is:

(a) An Activity (b) A process

(c) A Tradition (d) An Illusion

9. Management ensures:

(a) Providing employment opportunities

(b) Maintaining profit

(c) Ensuring maximum utilisation of resources

(d) Control on cost

10. Management is important because:

(a) It helps in achieving group goals

(b) It helps in development of society

(c) It increases efficiency

(d) All of the above

11. Which of the following has formalised methods of acquiring training and

experience?

(a) Management (b) Law

(c) Medical (d) All of these

12. Which of the following have no representative professional organisations

available?

(a) Law (b) Management

(c) Medical (d) Accountancy

13. Which degree is essential to become a manager?

(a) B.Com. (b) M.Com.

(c) M.B.A. (d) None of these

Multiple Choice Questions

5

14. For which of following minimum qualification has not been prescribed?

(a) Manager (b) Doctor

(c) Lawyer (d) Chartered Accountant

15. What is the name of the management institute established in India?

(a) IIT (b) AIMA

(c) IIM (d) ICICI

16. "Art is bringing about of a desired result through application of skill". Whose

statement is this?

(a) T.L. Massie (b) G.R. Terry

(c) Prof. Dalton E. McFarland (d) None of these

17. Whose speciality happens to be 'personal skill'?

(a) Profession (b) Art

(c) Science (d) None of these

18. Who said that management is a soft science?

(a) Ernest Dale (b) G.R. Terry

(c) Keynes (d) Fayol

19. The principles of Physics and Chemistry are stable. What is your opinion

about management?

(a) Stable (b) Unstable

(c) No principle is available (d) None of these

20. Management is a/an

(a) Art (b) Science

(c) Profession (d) All of the above

21. Name the country in which management is accepted as profession.

(a) America (b) Japan

(c) India (d) America and Japan

22. Management may be called which of the following science?

(a) Perfect Science (b) Physics

(c) Applied Science (d) Chemistry

23. Levels of management in an organisation serve as a __________ line among the

different managerial posts.

(a) Strong (b) Dividing

(c) Weak (d) Straight

Business Studies

6

24. A __________ chain is formed from the top-level management to the lower-level

management.

(a) Vertical (b) Thick

(c) Scalar (d) Small

25. At what level of management does the Chief Executive Officer operate?

(a) Top-level (b) Middle-level

(c) Lower-level (d) None of these

26. To which level of management do the managers of first-line belong?

(a) Lower-level (b) Middle - level

(c) Top-level (d) None of these

27. What is that area called where the non-managerial members work?

(a) Shopping Area (b) Showroom Area

(c) Platform Area (d) Factory Area

28. 'Thinking before doing', under which function of management is this

performed?

(a) Controlling (b) Directing

(c) Organising (d) Planning

29. Under what function of management does the determining of structure of roles

fall?

(a) Planning (b) Organising

(c) Directing (d) Controlling

30. Under what function of management does the work of filling posts with people

fall?

(a) Planning (b) Organising

(c) Staffing (d) Directing

31. Under what function of management does the 'corrective action' fall?

(a) Planning (b) Organising

(c) Directing (d) Controlling

32. What, out of the following, does not fall under directing?

(a) Planning (b) Supervision

(c) Leadership (d) Motivation

33. Number of levels of management are:

(a) one (b) two

(c) three (d) four

Multiple Choice Questions

7

34. Coordination is needed where the efforts of __________ persons are required?

(a) One person (b) Two persons

(c) Three persons (d) Many persons

35. "Coordination is not a separate function of management but it happens to be

the final truth of all functions." In what context this observation has been

made?

(a) Coordination is the essence of management

(b) Coordination is not established automatically

(c) Coordination is a continuously moving process

(d) None of these

36. Which of the following is true?

(a) Coordination is not equally important at all levels of management

(b) Coordination has no importance

(c) Coordination is equally important at all levels of management

(d) None of these

37. Cooperation means __________ .

(a) Desire to work jointly (b) Determining Activities

(c) Both the above (d) None of the above

38. To what function of management is coordination associated with?

(a) Planning (b) Organising

(c) Staffing, directing and controlling (d) All of these

39. What out of the following has been called the essence of management?

(a) Communication (b) Coordination

(c) Supervision (d) Leadership

40. What is the focus of attention when a manager is busy in planning activity?

(a) Coordination (b) Directing

(c) Controlling (d) Staffing

41. What information do we get about coordination through the medium of interdependence

of various processes?

(a) Meaning (b) Characteristics

(c) Need (d) None of these

42. The words cooperation and coordination are __________ .

(a) Opposite (b) Synonym

(c) Complementary (d) All the above

43. What contributes to the elimination of complexities of large-scale organisations?

(a) Planning (b) Directing

(c) Controlling (d) Coordination

WORKSHEET-I

Q1. From the following statements: Identify the feature or characteristics of management

1. An organisation has a set of simple and clearly stated basic goals which are the basic reason for its existence.

2. Different organisations have different goals.

3. A retail store wants to increase sales to maximize its profits

4. In order to be successful, an organisation must change itself and its goals according to the Needs of the environment.

5. McDonald's, the fast food giant made major changes in its menu to be able to survive in the Indian market.

6. Management can't be seen but its presence can be felt in the way the organisation functions.

7. The goal of The Spastics Society of India is to impart education to children with special needs.

8. Management unites the efforts of different individuals in the organisation towards achieving these goals.

9. The activities involved in managing an enterprise are common to all organisations whether economic, social or political.

10. A petrol pump needs to be managed as much as a hospital or a school.

11. What managers do in India, the USA, Germany or Japan is the same. How they do it may be quite different. This difference is due to the differences in culture, tradition and history.

12. The flow of input material and the technology for transforming this input into the desired output for consumption.

13. This is interlinked with both the management of work and the management of people.

14. It is a series of continuous, composite, but separate functions (planning, organising, directing, staffing and controlling). These functions are simultaneously performed by all managers all the time.

15. Smita at Namchi Designer Candles performs several different tasks in a single day. Some days she may spend more time in planning a future exhibition and on another day, she may spend time in sorting out an employee's problem.

16. The task of a manager consists of an ongoing series of functions.

17. Every member of the group has a different purpose for joining the organisation but as members of the organization they work towards fulfilling the common organizational goal.

18. This requires team work and coordination of individual effort in a common direction.

19. The effect of management is noticeable in an organization where targets are met according to plans, employees are happy and satisfied, and there is orderliness instead of chaos.

20. In a factory, a product is manufactured, in a garment store a customer's need is satisfied and in a hospital a patient is treated. Management translates work in terms of goals to be achieved and assigns the means to achieve it.

21. Despite all developments in technology "getting work done through people" is still a major task for the manager

22. It implies dealing with employees as individuals with diverse needs and behaviour;

23. The task of management is to make people work towards achieving the organisation's goals, by making their strengths effective and their weaknesses irrelevant.

Q2. From the following statements: - Identify if the manager is efficient or effective?

1. The aim of all managers.

2. Complete the given task but at a high cost.

3. Suppose, a company's target production is 5000 units in a year. To achieve this target the manager has to operate on double shifts due to power failure most of the time. The manager is able to produce 5000 units but at a higher production cost.

4. Cutting down cost but not achieving the target production

5. Achieve goals

Q3. From the following statements:- Identify the related Objective of Management

1. It has to achieve a variety of objectives in all areas considering the interest of all stakeholders Including, shareholders, employees, customers and the government

2. In order to survive, an organisation must earn enough revenues to cover costs

3. A business enterprise must consistently creating economic value for various constituents of Society.

4. This includes using environmental friendly methods of production, giving employment Opportunities to the disadvantaged sections of society and providing basic amenities like schools and crèches to employees.

5. People join an organisation to satisfy their diverse needs. Which vary from financial needs such As competitive salaries and perks, social needs such as peer recognition and higher level needs such as personal growth and development.

6. Management has to reconcile personal goals with organisational objectives for harmony in the organisation.

Q4. From the following statements:- Identify the related Importance of Management

1. The task of a manager is to give a common direction to the numerous individual efforts in achieving the overall goal of the organisation.

2. The aim of a manager is to reduce costs and increase productivity

3. Management helps people adapt to these changes so that the organisation is able to maintain its competitive edge

4. Through motivation and leadership the management helps individuals to develop team spirit, cooperation and commitment to group success.

5. Members are able to achieve personal goals while contributing to the overall organizational objective.

6. It helps to provide good quality products and services, creates employment opportunities, adopts new technology for the greater good of the people and leads the path towards growth and development

7. All organisations have to function in an environment which is constantly changing

Q5. From the following statements:- Identify the Nature of Management as science art or profession.

1. Management is the skilful and personal application of existing knowledge to achieve desired Results. It can be acquired through study, observation and experience.

2. Personal application of knowledge with ingenuity and creativity is required to practice the basic Principles learnt i.e. theoretical knowledge.

3. Experts in their respective areas have derived certain basic principles which are applicable to a particular form.

4. The day-to-day job of managing an enterprise is based on study, observation and Experience. There is a lot of literature available in various areas of management like marketing, finance and human resources which the manager has to specialise in.

5. A good manager works through a combination of practice, creativity, imagination, initiative and Innovation.

6. A manager applies this acquired knowledge in a personalized and skilful manner in the light of the realities of a given situation. He is involved in the activities of the organisation, studies critical situations and formulates his own theories for use in a given situation.

7. The best managers are committed and dedicated individuals; highly trained and educated, with Personal qualities such as ambition, self-motivation, creativity and imagination, a desire for development of the self and the organisation.

8. All management practices are based on the same set of principles; what distinguishes a successful manager from a less successful one is the ability to put these principles into practice.

Q6. From the following statements:- Identify the Levels of Management

1. They consist of the senior-most executives of the organisation as the chairman, the chief Executive officer, chief operating officer, president and vice-president. A team consisting of managers at Functional levels, heading finance, marketing etc. For example chief finance officer, vice president (marketing).

2. Their basic task is to integrate diverse elements and coordinate the activities of different Departments according to the overall objectives of the organisation.

3. Managers are responsible for the welfare and survival of the organisation

4. They formulate overall organisational goals and strategies

5. They directly oversee the efforts of the workforce.

6. Their authority and responsibility is limited according to the plans drawn by the top Management.

7. They interact with the actual work force and pass on instructions of the middle management to the workers.

8. The job of the top manager is complex and stressful, demanding long hours and commitment to the organisation.

9. They are responsible for implementing and controlling plans and strategies developed by top Management.

10. They ensure that their department has the necessary personnel, and assign necessary duties And responsibilities to them,

11. These managers co-operate with other departments for smooth functioning of the Organisation. At the same time they are responsible for all the activities of first line managers

12. Through their efforts quality of output is maintained, wastage of materials is minimised and Safety standards are maintained.

13. Link between top and lower level managers.

14. They are superior to the first line managers. They are usually known as division heads, Production manager.

Q7. From the following statements:- Identify the functions of management:

1. This implies setting goals in advance and developing a way of achieving them efficiently and effectively

2. Organising involves the grouping of the required tasks into manageable departments or work units and the establishment of authority and reporting relationships within the organisational hierarchy

3. Help in the accomplishment of work and promote both the efficiency of operations and the effectiveness of results.

4. It involves activities such as recruitment, selection, placement and training of personnel.

5. It is to make sure that the right people with the right qualifications are available at the right places and times to accomplish the goals of the organisation.

6. It involves leading, influencing and motivating employees to perform the tasks assigned to them.

7. The task involves establishing standards of performance, measuring current performance, comparing this with established standards and taking corrective action where any deviation is found.

Q8. From the following statements:- Identify the Characteristics of Coordination
1. It is the process of achieving unity of action among interdependent activities and departments of an organisation.
2. It gives a common focus to group effort to ensure that performance is as it was planned and scheduled
3. It acts as the binding force between departments and ensures that all action is aimed at achieving the goals of the organisation.
4. Is not a one-time function but a continuous process. It begins at the planning stage and continues till controlling
5. In the absence of coordination there is overlapping and chaos instead of harmony and integration of activities.
6. Middle level management coordinates with both the top level and first line managers. Operational level management coordinates the activities of its workers
7. Even where members of a department willingly cooperate and work, coordination gives a direction to that willing spirit.

Q9. From the following statements:- Identify the Importance of Coordination
1. For organisational efficiency, it is important to harmonise individual goals and organisational goals through coordination.
2. The marketing department's objective may be to increase sales by 10 per cent by offering discounts. But, the finance department may not approve of such discounts as it means loss of revenue.
3. All departments and individuals are interdependent and they have to depend on each other for information to perform their activities
4. Modern organisations due to complexities of modern technology and the diversity of tasks to be performed, need to employ a number of specialists

<u>WORKSHEET-2</u>

1. Fl in the blanks:
a…………………….focuses on achieving goals.

b. ....focuses on reducing costs.

2. Identify the features of management in each of these lines:
a. Managers in India do the same work as managers in USA or Japan
b. Effect of management is noticeable in organisation where work is in order and employees are happy.
C.Management requires team work and coordination of individuals efforts towards organisation goals
d Mc Donalds made major changes in their food menu to survive in Indian markets.
e. The task of manager consists of ongoing series of functions.
f. Every organisation has a set of goals. For example, goal of a retail store is to increase in its sales
g Management is complex activity and has three dimensions

3. identify the objectives in each of the statement given below
a Rooftop meetings friendly coworkers and team-oriented environment are part of work culture of twitter
B.Starbucks aims at creating a product that is not only beneficial to its customers but also to the environment.
C An organisation needs to survive earn profits and grow
d. The task of manager is to give common direction to individual effort in achieving overall goal of the organisation.
e. Through motivation and leadership, management helps to develop team spirit, cooperation and commitment to group success.

4. Identify the function of management in each of the statement given below:
 a. Finding deviations between actual and planned performance:
b. Leading, influencing and motivating employees of organisation:
C. Recruitment, selection and training of personnel:
d. Bridging the gap between where we are and where we want to go:
e. Division of work, departmentalisation, assignment of tasks and creating reporting relationships:

5. identify the importance of management:
a. The aim of manager is to reduce costs and increase productivity.
 b. Management helps to provide good quality products and services and creating employment opportunities.
C. Management helps people to adapt to changes so that organisation is able to maintain its competitive edge.
d. the task of the manager is to give common direction to individual effort in achieving overall organization goals.
e. through motivation and leadership, management helps to develop team spirit, cooperation and commitment to group success.

6. State the level of management at which each of the following is working:
a. Operations manager.
b. Vice president
C. Plant superintendent:
d. Foreman

e. Section officer
f. Marketing manager.
g. Division head:

7. Identify point of importance of coordination in each of the following:
 a. Coordination is required to reconcile the differences in approach, opinion and interest of different specialists.
 b. It is important to harmonise individual goals and organisational goals through coordination
 C. The process of linking the activities of different departments is accomplished by coordination.

8. Identify the features of coordination in each of these lines
a. It begins at planning stage and continues till controlling stage
b it acts as a binding force between departments
c. It is required in all departments of an organisation
d it unifies diverse interests into purposeful work activity

9 "Management is a series of continuous interrelated functions" Explain

10. Meera argues that management is an art but Shubham says that management is a science. What do you think who's right? Also, give reasons with their explanations.

11 "Coordination is the essence of management Explain the statement

12. Do you think management has the characteristics of a full-fledged profession? Give reasons

<u>WORKSHEET-3</u>

1. Identify the feature or characteristics of management from the following statements:

I.   McDonalds made major changes in its menu to be able to survive in the Indian market .It offers 'Aloo Tikki Burger' to attract Indian customers.

II.   An organization consists of diverse individuals with different needs.

III.   Management functions (planning, organising, directing, staffing and controlling) are simultaneously performed by all managers all the time

IV.   This requires a production process which entails the flow of input material and the technology for transforming this input into the desired output for consumption.

V.   It integrates the efforts of all members towards achieving the objectives.

VI.   Management requires team work and coordination of individual effort in a common direction.

VII.   Managers in India do the same work as managers in USA or Japan or Germany

VIII.   Management consists of ongoing series of functions.

IX.   An organisation has a set of basic goals like the goal of retail store is to increase sale
X.   In an organization employees are happy & satisfied & no chaos exists.
XI.   Management is to be seen in business & non business organizations
XII.   Management translates this work in terms of goals to be achieved and assigns the means to achieve it.
XIII.   With the introduction of per second call by a cellular company, other cellular companies also started offering per second calls to maintain market share.
XIV.   A petrol pump needs to be managed as much as a hospital or a school
XV.   Effect of management can always be noticed in every successful & unsuccessful organization.
XVI.   Managerial activities are performed in all types of organizations in all departments at all levels.

2. Is the manager efficient or effective?

I.   A company's target production is 10,000 units in a year, to achieve this target the manager has to operate in double shifts due to power failure. The manager is able to meet the target but at a higher production cost.
II.   Manager concentrate more on producing goods with fewer resources i.e., cutting down cost but not achieving the target production.
III.   Sales manager was given target to make sales of 1000 units in a month. He achieved the target but he gave more discounts to customers which reduced company's profit.
IV.   Rajat is HR Manager in ABC Ltd. He had to arrange for recruitment and selection of 100 workers to meet an urgent order within a week .He was able to appoint only 80 workers in 15 days.

2. Identify the objective of management from the following statements:

I.   A company uses environmental friendly methods of production.
II.   Asian paints contributed a large amount of funds to enable farmers to use their local resources
III.   Management provides competitive salaries & perks.
IV.   To meet the objectives of the firm the management of Angora Ltd. Offer employment to physically challenged persons
V.   Management offers employment to physically challenged people.
VI.   The revenue generated by a firm is just sufficient to cover the cost of production.

VII.   Management provides peer recognition.
VIII.   Generate employment opportunities for weaker section of society.
IX.   A business needs to add to its prospects in the long run.
X.   Management provides for personal growth & development of employee.
XI.   Through e-chaupal, ITC aims to change the quality of life & the entire
         outlook of the Indian farmers.
XII.   For every classmate notebook u buy,IT C contributes Rs.1 to its rural dev
         initiative that supports primary education in villages

3.   Identify the different levels of management in the following cases:

I.   Aashi is the manager of the northern division of a large corporate house
II.   Mr Sagar determines the overall objectives & strategies for the organization.
III.   Ramesh interacts with the actual work force.
IV.   Mr Ajit Shrivastav act as a conduit .
V.   Aditya is responsible for framing the plans & policies of AB industries.
VI.   Mehul interpret the policies framed by top management
VII.   Harish is a plant superintendent in the cargo co.
VIII.   Sarvesh Ensures interdepartmental cooperation
IX.   Suresh is working as Plant Superintendent in Surat
X.   Dinesh is working as 'operations manager' in Tifco ltd.
XI.   Tanvir is responsible for assigning work to employees & representing their
         grievances to his boss
XII.   Mr Robinson analyse the business environment and its implications for the
         survival of the firm.
XIII.   Prabhu decides opening a new branch of the business.
XIV.   Raman is responsible for the welfare & survival of the organization.
XV.   Tapasya is responsible for implementing & controlling the plans & strategies
         of the organization.
XVI.   Dinesh is a superintendent in a cargo co.
XVII.   Ram is working as a regional manager

4. Identify the nature of management

I.   Management is a systematized body of knowledge that explain certain
        general truths.
II.   It is practiced as personal application of existing theoretical knowledge in
        one's own unique manner.

III. There has been an increase in the corporate form of business & increasing emphasis on managed business concern.
IV. All management practices are based on the same set of principles; what distinguishes a successful manager from a less successful one is the ability to put these principles into practice
V. Management scholars like F.W. Taylor and Henri Fayol have been able to identify general principles of management.
VI. There are several associations of practising managers in India, like the AIMA (All India Management Association) that has laid down a code of conduct to regulate the activities of their members.

5. Identify the functions of management:

I. Leading, influencing & motivating employees to perform the tasks assigned to them.
II. It involves monitoring organisational performance towards the attainment of organisational goals.
III. It involves the grouping of the required tasks into manageable departments or work units and the establishment of authority and reporting relationships within the organisational hierarchy
IV. Finding out deficiencies in implementation of plans with the result achieved.
V. Deciding the objectives, policies & procedures to be followed in the company.
VI. Assigning duties grouping tasks, establishing authority & allocating resources required to carry out a specific plan.
VII. Recruitment & selection of the personnel.
VIII. Discrepancies between actual and realized activities are taken care at this stage

6. Identify the point of importance of management from following statements:

I. An organisation has multiple objectives to serve the purpose of the different groups that constitute it
II. Management helps people adapt to these changes so that the organisation is able to maintain its competitive edge
III. The aim of a manager is to reduce costs and increase productivity
IV. A manager motivates and leads his team in such a manner that individual members are able to achieve personal goals while contributing to the overall organisational objective.

V.   The task of a manager is to give a common direction to the individual effort in achieving the overall goal of the organisation

VI.   Management helps to provide good quality products and services, creates employment opportunities etc.

Case Studies

Q1. Delhi CM Mr. Arvind Kejriwal launched Odd Even rule for cars in Delhi to cut pollution by restricting the number of cars running on city road.

a) Identify and explain the objective of Management highlighted by our Chief Minister in the above case.

Q2. Mrs. Wason passed her MBBS examination and also passed MS examination as an eye specialist. After 2 years of completing her studies she joined a big hospital as an eye surgeon. Now she is performing successfully since last few years. Mr. Madan founder of CTA feels that Mrs. Wason is experiencing the aspect of science and Ms. Sachdeva feels that she is experiencing the aspect of Art. Who is right? Give reasons in support of your answer.

Q3 Shiv Nadar, chairman and CEO of HCL attributes the success of the group to its management team and their entrepreneurial spirit which together have enabled it to handle rapid changes in the environment and technologies. At HCL management believes that happy, satisfied and self motivated employees help in reducing costs and increase productivity. It also has a strong sense of social responsibility and has set up educational institutions in the field of management, engineering, computers etc.

Identify and explain the significance of understanding management by quoting relevant lines from the case study.

.

Q4 Raman agreed to be an employee of a company on the condition that he will be given a project offering competitive salary, career advancement opportunity, promotion and recognition. Mr. John, (general manager) puts Raman in a project in which promotion is not possible. Raman gets disheartened and feels frustrated all the time. Such frustration also reflected in his work and he could not bring desired results.

(a) Which objective of management Raman could not achieve? Explain.

(b) Identify the other two objectives.

(c) What should Mr. John do to avoid such problem?

Q5 Vineet joined a company after completing graduation in management from a reputed business school. During his induction training, he was informed that he would be working in production department. The company wanted to achieve 30% increase in output in the next quarter. His general manager, a man with decades of experience, also said that management is a complex activity. He expected Vineet to make production plans, identify incentive schemes for workers to make their strengths effective and ensure that there is no disruption due to technical glitch. Vineet realised very quickly that his job is a series of continuous tasks. After one month, he was informed by the general manager that due to increase in international demand, production targets have been raised.

He called an urgent meeting of his supervisors and senior workers. He offered them an opportunity to realise their potential and earn more by working overtime and in multiple shifts. He was delighted that at the end of the quarter, he was able to meet the targets, workers were

happy and there was no chaos.
Identify and explain any four characteristics of management referred in above case.

Q6 The production manager assigned a target of producing 1,000 TV sets in the month of October among the group of 10 workers. They mutually decided to produce 100 TV sets each. Among them 3 of the workers of the group fell sick. The other worker refused to divide his work among and concentrated only on the production of their own individual target of production the group target of 1,000 TV sets could not be achieved..
(i)Which characteristic of management is violated in the above para?

Q7 XYZ Power Ltd. Set up a factory for manufacturing solar lanterns in a remote village as there was no reliable supply of electricity in rural areas. They revenue earned by the company was sufficient to cover the costs and the risks. The demand of the lanterns was increasing day-by-day. So the company decided to increase production to generate higher sales. For this, they decided to employ people from the nearby villages as very few job opportunities were available in that area. They company also decided to open school and creches for the children of its employees.
(i) Identify and explain the objectives of management discussed above.
(ii) State any two values which the company wanted to communicate to the society.

Q8 Kamal, Khan and Devid are partners in a firm engaged in the distribution of dairy products in Madhya Pradesh. Kamal is a holder of Senior Secondary School Certificate from Central Board of Secondary Education with Business Studies as one of his elective subjects. Khan had done his post-graduation in Hindi literature and Devid in Dairy Farming. One day there was a serious discussion between Khan and Devid regarding the nature of 'Management as a Science'. Khan argued that Management was not a science whereas Devid was of the opinion that Management was a science. Kamal intervened and corrected both Khan and Devid about the nature of Management as a Science with the help of his knowledge of Business Studies. Explain, how Kamal would have been able to satisfy both Khan and Devid.

Q9 Shahrukh Khan is an epitome of success. He adds humour and humane touch in his performances at the live shows. He has redefined the image of a lead actor in cinema and given it a 'negative, sympathetic and glamorous look'. A manager also redefines and creates styles and techniques based on his experience and imagination. Identify the nature of management form the given statement

Q10 Alia Enterprises, a company was initially producing grinders and mixers. Now, with the changing scenario and emerging trends of working women there is a greater demand for a product which is more efficient and a multi-tasker. On analyzing the situation, the company decided to penetrate into the market for producing Food Processor. Which level of management will take this decision?

Q11 Sushil is running a business enterprise producing handloom and handicraft products in Maharashtra under the name 'Fabmart Enterprises'. He has employed 1,000 craftsmen and artisans in his firm. The basic reason for its existence is to produce those handicraft items which have a market demand & are reasonably priced. He performs all the functions of management all the time with the help of his managers. He is working with a team of individuals who have diverse needs and goals. He along with his marketing experts conducts market survey to know the tastes and preferences of consumers. Thus he adapts to changing environment and produces goods according to the needs of the customers. The employees working in his firm are happy and satisfied, and there is orderliness instead of chaos.

Identify any five features of management from the above para. Also quote lines that denote these features

Q12 Amar Ltd.is engaged in production of electrical goods The company's profits and market share are declining. The production department blames the marketing department for not meeting the sales targets and the marketing department blames the production department for producing goods which are not of good quality and do not meet the customer's expectations. The finance department blames both the production and marketing departments for declining return on investment.

1.What quality of management do you think the company is lacking?

2.List its two features

3.List any two values which are ignored by employees of Amar Ltd.

Q13 What distinguishes a successful manager from less successful manager is ability to put the principles and methods of management into practice .What aspect of nature of management is being highlighted here.

Case Studies Solution

1. Social Objective (with explanation)
2. Both are right

   Mrs. Wason is experiencing the aspect of science - Mrs. Wason passed her MBBS examination and also passed MS examination as an eye specialist.

   Ms. Sachdeva is experiencing the aspect of Art. - After 2 years of completing her studies she joined a big hospital as an eye surgeon. Now she is performing successfully since last few years.

3.

Point of Significance of understanding management	Line quoted	Explanation
Creates Dynamic organization	Shiv Nadar, chairman and CEO ………. Environment and technologies	Management helps the employees overcome their resistance to change and adapt as per changing situation to ensure its survival and growth
Increases Efficiency	At HCL management believes that………..increase productivity	Management increases efficiency by using resources in the best possible manner to reduce cost and increase productivity.
Development of Society	It also has a strong sense of ……….engineering, computers etc.	Management helps in the development of society by producing good quality products, creating employment opportunities and adopting new technology.

4.

(a) Objective of management that could not achieved is <u>Personal objectives</u> (with explanation)
(b) The other two objectives. (With explanation)
* Economic objectives
* Social objectives
(c) Mr. John should try to bring balanace between personal and economic objectives.

5 Four characteristics of management referred in given case
* <u>Goal oriented Process</u> It is a goal oriented process, which is undertaken to achieve already specified and desired objectives by proper utilization of available resources.
* <u>Continuous:</u> It consists of a series of function and its functions are being performed by all managers simultaneously. The process of management continues till an organization exists for attaining its objectives.
* .<u>Multidimensional:</u> It is multidimensional as it involves management of work, people and operations. It is complex activity
* <u>Intangible Force</u> : It is intangible force as it can't be seen but its effects can be felt in the form of results like whether the objectives are met and whether people are motivated or not and there is orderliness and coordination in the work environment.

6. Characteristic of management is violated in the given para is <u>management is Group Activity</u>

7. (i) The objectives of management discussed are (with explanation)

* Economic objectives
* Social objectives
(ii) Two values which the company wanted to communicate to the society:

* Concern for society
* Generation of employment

8. Management as a Science
Science is a systematised body of knowledge that is based on general truths which can be tested anywhere, anytime.
The features of Science are as follows:

(1) Systematized body of knowledge: Science has a systematized body of knowledge based on principles and experiments.
(2) Principles based on experiments and observation: Scientific principles are developed through experiments and observation.
(3) Universal validity: Scientific principles have universal validity and application.

Management has systematic body of knowledge and its principles are developed over a period of time based on repeated experiments & observations which are universally applicable but they have to be modified according to given situation. As the principles of management are not as exact as the principles of pure science, so it may be called-an inexact science. The prominence of human factor in the management makes it a Social Science.

9. The nature of management form the given statement   is <u>management as an art</u>

10. Level of management that will take this decision is <u>Top Level</u>

11.

Feature of management	Line quoted
Goal oriented	The basic reason for …….. reasonably priced.
Continuous	He performs all the functions of management all the time with the help of his managers.
Dynamic	Thus he adapts to changing environment and produces goods according to the needs of the customers.
Group Activity	He is working with a team of individuals who have diverse needs and goals
Intangible	The employees working in his firm are happy and satisfied, and there is orderliness instead of chaos

12.

1 Quality of management that company is lacking is coordination

2. Features of coordination are (Any two)

- Coordination integrates group effort.
- Coordination ensures unity of action
- Coordination is a continuous process
- Coordination is all pervasive function
- Coordination is the responsibility of all managers
- Coordination is a deliberate function

3. Two values which are ignored by employees of Amar Ltd.
    o Cooperation
    o Concern for organisational objectives

14. Nature of management is being highlighted here is <u>management as an Art</u>

LATEST CBSE QUESTIONS

1. Question 1:Ashutosh Goenka was working in 'Axe Ltd.', a company manufacturing air purifiers. He found that the profits has started declining from the last six months. Profit has an implication for the survival of the firm, so he analysed the business environment to find out the reasons for this decline. Identify the level of management at which Ashutosh Goenka was working. State three other functions being performed by Ashutosh Goenka.
Answer: Ashutosh Goenka was working at top level of management. The three functions being performed by him at this level are outlined below:
1.He is responsible for formulating the overall organizational goals and strategies.
2. He is responsible for all the business activities and its impact on society.
3. He has to coordinate the activities of different departments in pursuit of common goals.

Question 2: Rishitosh Mukerjee has recently joined AMV Ltd, a company manufacturing refrigerators. He found that his department was under-staffed and other departments were not cooperating with his deparment for smooth functioning of the organisation. Therefore, he ensured that his department has the required number of employees and its cooperation with other deparments is improved.

1. Idenfity the level at which Rishitosh Mukerjee was working.
2. Also, state three more functions required to be performed by Rishitosh Mukerjee at
3. this level.

Answer: Rishitosh Mukerjee is working at middle level of the management. The three more functions that he has to perform at this level are stated below:

1. He has to assign duties and responsibilities to the people in his department.
2. He has to motivate the people in his department to achieve the desired objectives.
3. He has to interpret the policies framed by top management.

Question 3: Sridhar's father is working as a section in-charge in a government office. Identify the level of management at which he is working? State any five functions that he has to perform at this level.

Answer: Sridhar's father is working as a section in-charge in a government office. He is working at the lower level of management.He has to perform the following functions at this level of management:

1. He has to directly oversee the efforts of the workforce.
2. He has to serve as a link between the workers and middle level managers.
3. He has to ensure sufficient availability of resources and good quality of output.
4. He has to provide guidance and training to workers.
5. He has to ensure that good working conditions are provided to the workers.

Question 4: Mega Ltd. manufactured water-heaters. In the first year of its operations, the revenue earned by the company was just sufficient to meet its costs. To increase the revenue, the company analysed the reasons behind the less revenues. After analysis, the company decided:

1. to reduce the labour costs by shifting the manufacturing unit to a backward area where labour was available at a very low rate.
2. to start manufacturing solar water-heaters and reduce the production of electric water- heaters slowly.This will not only help in covering the risks but also help in meeting other objectives.

1. Identify and explain the objectives of management discussed above.
2. State any two values which the company wanted to communicate to society.

Answer:

1. The objectives of management discussed above are:
   - Organisational objectives: An organisation strives to achieve multiple organizational objectives in the interest of its stakeholders like

owners, employees etc.The main organizational objectives are survival, profit and growth.
- Social Objectives: It is the obligation of every organisation to undertake such activities which will benefit the society at large like using eco-friendly methods, contributing towards weaker sections of the society, generating employment opportunities, promoting literacy etc.

2. The two values that the company wanted to communicate to the society are:
   - Rural development
   - Environment sustainability

Question 5:XYZ Power Ltd. set up a factory for manufacturing solar lanterns in a remote village as there was no reliable supply of electricity in rural areas. The revenue earned by the company was sufficient to cover the costs and the risks. As the demand of lanterns was increasing day- by-day, the company decided to increase production to generate higher sales. For this/they decided to employ people from a nearby village as very few job opportunities were available in that area. The company also decided to open schools and creches for the children of its employees.

1. Identify and explain the objectives of management discussed above.
2. State any two values which the company wanted to communicate to the society.

Answer:

1. The objectives of management discussed above are:
   - Organisational objectives: An organisation strives to achieve multiple organizational objectives in the interest of its stakeholders

like owners, employees etc. The main organisational objectives are survival, profit and growth.

- Social Objectives: It is the obligation of every organisation to undertake such activities which will benefit the society at large like using eco-friendly methods, contributing towards weaker sections of the society, generating employment opportunities, promoting literacy etc.

2. The two values that the company wanted to communicate to the society are:

- Rural development
- Promoting literacy

Question 6: Your grandfather has retired as the Director of a manufacturing company. At what level of management was he working? What functions do you think he was performing at that level? State any two,

Answer:: Since he has retired from the post of Director of a manufacturing company, he was working at the top level of management. The main functions that he was performing at this level are outlined below:

1. He was responsible for the success and failure of the organization.
2. He was responsible for all the business activities and its impact on society.
3. He had to coordinate the activities of different departments in pursuit of common goals.

Question 7: Ritu is the manager of the northern division of a large corporate house. At what level does she work in the organisation? What are her basic functions?

OR

Your grandfather has retired from an organisation in which he was responsible for implementing the plans developed by the top management. At which level of management was he working? State one more function performed at this level.

OR

Deepak's father has retired as a purchase manager of a company. At what level of management was he working? What function do you think he was performing at that level of management?

OR

Dheeraj is working as an Operations Manager in Tifco Ltd. Name the managerial level at which he is working. State any four functions he will perform as the Operations Manager in this company.

OR

Rajat is working as a Regional Manager in Tifco Ltd. Name the level at which he is working. State any four functions he will perform as the Regional Manager in this company.

Answer:: Ritu / grandfather / Deepak's father / Deeraj / Rajat, all of them are working at the middle level of management.

The four functions that he will have to perform at this level are stated below:

1. He has to ensure that his department has the necessary staff.
2. He has to assign duties and responsibilities to the people in his department.
3. He has to motivate the people in his department to achieve the desired objectives.
4. He has to co-operate with the other departments for ensuring smooth functioning of the organization.

Question 8:

Vaibhav Garments Ltd/s target is to produce 10,000 shirts per month at a cost of ?150 per shirt. The production manager could achieve this target at the cost of ?160 per shirt. Do you think the production manager is effective? Give reasons for your answer.

Answer:

Yes, the production manager of Vaibhav Garments Ltd. is effective as he could achieve the target to produce 10,000 shirts in a month.

Mr. Nitin Singhania's father has a good business of iron and steel. He wants to go to the USA for his MBA but his father thinks that he should join the business. On the basis of emerging- trends, do you think that Mr. Singhania should send his son to the USA? Give any three reasons in support of your answer.

Yes, according to me, Mr. Singhania should send his son to USA for his MBA because management is being recognised as a profession to a great extent because of the following reasons:

1. Well defined body of knowledge: Management is considered to be a well-defined body of knowledge that can be acquired through instructions. As a separate discipline, it contains a set of theories and principles formulated by various management experts. Moreover, it is taught in various schools and colleges all over the world.
2. Ethical code of conduct: Management, in practice, like other professions, is bound by a code of conduct which guides the behaviour of its members. Therefore, acquiring a degree in management will equip him with the good managerial,, skills and approach.

3. Service motive: A good management course will provide him an insight into the multiple goals that an organisation should pursue. This knowledge will help him to serve both the objectives of profit maximization and social welfare effectively for his company.

NCERT Solutions

Short Answers Type

Question 1: Define Management.

Solution : Management can be defined as a process of getting the work or the task done that is required for achieving the goals of an organisation in an efficient and effective manner.

Process implies the functions of the management. That is, planning, organising, staffing, directing and controlling. On the other hand, effective implies completing the given task and work while, efficient means successfully completing the task with minimum possible cost. The various functions of a management suggests that a manager first plans, then organises, puts staff in position, then directs, and finally controls.

Management is important because it helps in achieving group goals, increases efficiency, creates a dynamic organisation, helps achieve personal objectives and contributes to the development of society.

Management is a combination of an organised body of knowledge (science) and its skillful application (art). Although it does not satisfy all the requirements of a profession, it is to a large extent professional in character.

Management is considered a three-tier activity. The top management focuses on determination of objectives and policies, middle management attempts to achieve these objectives through the effort of other managers and supervisory or operational management directly oversees the efforts of the workforce

Question 2 : Name any two important characteristics of management.
Solution :

The following are the two characteristics of management.

i. *Pervasive*- Management is pervasive to all organizations across size, characteristics and region.

That is, all organizations whether large or small, working whether for economic, social or political interest and in any region need management. For example, a corporate firm requires management as does a non-profit organisation. Similarly, a hotel needs as much management as a hospital. In addition, management is practiced by organizations in all the countries and regions. The only difference lies in how it is practiced by different organizations in different regions based on their culture and traditions.

ii. *Continuous Process*- Management is a continuous process. That is, the various functions of management (planning, organising, directing, staffing and controlling) are performed simultaneously by the managers. However, the focus or the priority of the manager may differ from day to day. While on one day, the manger mat devotes more time towards planning, while on other day more time may be spent on controlling.

Question 3 : Ritu is the manager of the northern division of a large corporate house. At what level does she work in the organisation? What are the basic functions?
   Solution : Ritu being the manager of the northern division of the organisation is in the middle-level management. She and other mangers like her act as a link between the top management and the operational management. Her main task is to oversee the implementation of the plans and policies formulated by the top management by directing and supervising the functions of the lower management.

The following are her basic functions.

1. Interpreting the policies formulated by the top management.
2. To make sure that each department under her division has the required personnel and staff for carrying out the assigned work.
3. To assign the necessary duties and responsibilities to the persons working in various departments.
4. To encourage and motivate the personnel towards achieving the goals.
5. Co-operate with other departments for smooth functioning of the organisation.

Question 4: Why is management considered a multi-faced concept?
Solution :

Management is said to be multi-faceted concept as it is a complex process involving not just one but various dimensions. There are three main dimensions of management.

i. *Managing the Work*- The performance of a definite work forms the basis of an organisation. With management this work is interpreted in terms of the objectives and goals and how they are to be achieved. The task of management is to make people work towards achieving the organization's goals, by making their strengths effective and their weaknesses irrelevant.

ii. *Managing the People*- As the work is to be done by the people, managing the people is another important dimension of management. It involves dealing with the employees both as an individual and as groups or teams. With management their strengths are utilised and weakness are worked upon so as to achieve the desired objectives.

iii. *Managing the Operations-* Every organisation involves a production process where the inputs are transformed into a product or a service. This production process requires continuous management. Thus, we can say that management is a multi-dimensional process .

Question 5 : Discuss the basic features of management as a profession.
Solution :

The following are the basic features according to which management can be viewed as a profession.

i. *Systemised Knowledge-* Management is based on a systemised and well-defined body of knowledge comprising of principles and theories. This knowledge can be attained through various colleges, institutes and books.

ii. *Professional Association-* As every profession, management is also affiliated to a professional association that regulates the functions of the members. For example, in India the AIMA (All India Management Association) regulates the functioning of its member managers. However, there is no compulsion for every manager to be member of the association.

iii. *Restriction to Entry-* Although no specific qualifications or degrees are required to be a manger, however, professional knowledge in terms of management degrees and diplomas are preferred. To some extent, this restricts the entry of people in management as a profession.

iv. *Code of Conduct-* Every profession follows a particular code of conduct that acts as a guiding principle for the ethical behavior of its members. Through good management, the production takes place in an effective and efficient manner and quality goods and services are provided to the society at a fair price.

Long Answer Type
Question 1 : Management is considered to be both an art and a science. Explain.
Solution :

Management fulfills the criteria of both an art as well as a science. The following points explain the features of management as an art and as a science.

Management as an Art

Art is the skillful and personal application of existing knowledge to achieve desired results. It can be acquired through study, observation and experience. Since art is concerned with personal application of knowledge some kind of ingenuity and creativity is required to practice the basic principles learnt. Management satisfies the following criteria for it to be called an art.

i. *Existence of Theoretical Knowledge*: Art presupposes the existence of certain theoretical knowledge. Experts in their respective areas have derived certain basic principles which are applicable to a particular form of art. Various theories and principles have been developed in management. Such as Henry Fayol's Principles of Management, Taylor's Scientific Management Theory.

ii. *Personalised Application*: Art is the personalised concept. That is, each individual uses the basic knowledge in his own creative way. For example, every dance form has some basic steps. These steps are used by each dancer using his own creative manner. In a similar manner, managers use the available theories and principles as per the situation in their own unique manner. That is, the managers use their own creativity and imagination for the application of the knowledge of management.

iii. ***Based on Practice and Creativity***: Art involves practice and innovation. The artists use the existing literature as per his own creativity and innovation. For example, two writers can describe a given situation based on their unique interpretations. Similarly, in management, a manager applies the theories and principles of management to different situations as per his own creativity and imagination and sometimes even formulates new ways to address a situation.

Management as a Science

Science is a systematized body of knowledge that explains certain general truths or the operation of general laws. As a science, management fulfills the following criteria.

i. ***Systematic Body of Knowledge***: Science has a specified body of knowledge which is based on cause and effect relationship. Similarly, management has its own body of theories and principles that are developed over years. For example, all of us discuss sports like cricket and soccer using a common vocabulary. The players also use these terms to communicate with each other. Similarly managers need to communicate with one another with the help of a common vocabulary for a better understanding of their work situation.

ii. ***Principles Based on Experimentation***: In science the principles and theories are based on continuous observation and experimentation. In a same manner, the principles of management have also developed over several years based on repeated observations and experiments. However, as against science, in management no exact cause and effect relationship can be established. This is because management primarily deals with humans and human behavior. As human behavior is subject change, so, the outcome of these theories would also vary from one situation to another. Despite this, management fulfils this criterion of science to some extent as the scholars have been able to identify certain theories and principle that act as guidelines in management.

iii. ***Universal Validity***: In science, the principles have universal validity. In management also the theories and principles are valid to some extent if not universal. Although the application of the theories and their outcomes vary from situation to situation, however they act as standards for actions in different situations. That is, these principles can be used for the basic training of the managers.

**Question 2 : Do you think management has the characteristics of a full fledged profession?
Solution :**

Although management does not satisfy all the criteria of a profession, however, it does posses some of the characteristics that qualify it to be a profession.

The following are the characteristics of management as a profession.

i. *Well defined body of Knowledge*- Management has a systemised and well-defined body of knowledge. It is based on several theories and principles that are developed over years with continuous experimentation and observation. The knowledge of management can be attained through various colleges, institutes and books. Management as a course is offered by many colleges and professional institutes. For example, in India, the Indian Institute of Management (IIM) is the premier institute of management.

ii. *Restriction to Entry*- Management satisfies this criterion only to some extent. As against other professions such a doctor or a lawyer, no specific qualification or degree are required to be a manager. That is, any person holding any degree or qualification can be a manager. However, the entry is restricted as persons with professional management degree or diploma are preferred.

iii. *Professional Association-* A professional has to be a member or should be associated with a statutory body which is responsible for stating the laws and authorities of that profession. Management is affiliated to a professional association that regulates the functions of the members. In India, the AIMA (All India Management Association) is an association for the managers. But, it is not requisite for managers to be a part of them.

iv. *Motive*: The basic purpose of management is to help the organisation achieve its stated goal. This may be profit maximisation for a business enterprise and service for a hospital. However, profit maximisation as the objective of management does not hold true and is fast changing. Therefore, if an organisation has a good management team that is efficient and effective it automatically serves society by providing good quality products at reasonable prices.

Thus, it can be said that to some extent management satisfies the criterion for it to be called a profession.

Question 3: Coordination is the essence of management. Do you agree? Give reasons.
Solution :

Yes, Coordination is indeed the essence of management. By Coordination, we mean a path through which the group functions are linked up. It binds the people of the organisation and their activities to ensure a smooth functioning of the work. It is that force which unites the working and efforts of the people of the organisation towards the common objective of the organisation. Coordination links the interrelated functions of management. It is found at every level of management. It begins right from the stage of planning where goals and objectives are set for the organisation. Coordination is then required between the stage of planning and staffing so that right kind of people are hired for the execution of the plan. Next the functions of directing and controlling must also be coordinated with each other so as to realise the achievement of desired goals.

The following points highlight the importance of coordination in management.

(a) *Harmonized Goals*: In any organisation, growth is one of important goals. With growth of the organisation, its size increases and the number of personnel also increases. However, greater number of persons means more differences in thoughts and work habits that may lead to disharmony among people. Also, every individual will have his/her personal goals which may create hindrance in achieving the organizational goals. So, coordination is important so as to synchronize the personal and the overall goals in one direction.

(b) *Allotted Work*: Each task requires specialisation to give the requisite results. For this, every organisation hires expert for different tasks. Every specialist approaches the tasks in his own unique manner and is generally reluctant to take up any advice or suggestion form others. This may lead to diversion or conflict among various specialists in the organisation. Thus, coordination is required from an outside body such as the manager so as to integrate their opinions and thoughts.

(c) *Interdependence of Divisions*: An organisation has various departments and sub-departments such as production, sales, finance, etc. Every department works independently and with its own policies and objectives. For example, the sales department may want greater monetary incentives for its employees but the finance department may not approve of such incentives as it may lead to increase in the cost of the organisation. In this case, there arises a conflict between the two departments. Thus, here also coordination is needed to synchronize the activities of each department towards the achievement of common goals of the organisation. Hence, we see that coordination is intrinsic and imperative for management. It is the 'essence' of management.

Question 4 : "A successful enterprise has to achieve its goals effectively and efficiently." Explain.

Solution :

Management is defined as a process of getting the work or the task done that is required for achieving the goals of an organisation in an efficient and effective manner. Here, the two key words- efficient and effective play an important role.

Effectiveness means completing the given work in the required time. In other words, it means doing the right things with focus on the end result. It is a very important aspect of management as it helps in reaching the set goals. Efficiency on the other hand, means completing the task with minimum possible costs and resources. Efficiency is said to increase if greater benefits are achieved using lesser resources or even if same benefits can be derived by cutting down on resources. Suppose, a company's target production is 5000 units in a year. To achieve this target the manager has to operate on double shifts due to power failure most of the time. The manager is able to produce 5000 units but at a higher production cost. In this case, the manager was effective but not so efficient, since for the same output, more inputs (labour cost, electricity costs) were used. At times, a business may concentrate more on producing goods with fewer resources i.e., cutting down cost but not achieving the target production. Consequently, the goods do not reach the market and hence the demand for them declines and competitors enter the market. This is a case of being efficient but not effective since the goods did not reach the market.

For an organisation, both effectiveness and efficiency play an equally important role in achieving the goals. While on one hand, being effective implies actually achieving the goals, on the other hand, being efficient would reduce the cost and thereby, increase profits. However, often an organisation has to compromise on one while achieving the other. That is, if the company focuses on effectiveness, it may have to compromise on efficiency and vice-versa. For example, suppose to complete a given task of production, the manager decides to hire more number of workers. This would mean that he will have to give more salary which in turn increases the total cost of production. In this case, the manager may complete the allotted task in time but the task would lack efficiency. On the other hand, if the manger continues to work with the available workers so as not to increase the cost, then this would result in the delay of the project. That is, in this case the manager compromises on effectiveness while achieving efficiency.

Hence, it is necessary to maintain a balance between effectiveness and efficiency. Undue emphasis on one without the other is of no good for the organisation.

Question 5: Management is a series of continuous interrelated functions. Comment.
Solution :

In the words of 'Robert L. Trewelly and M. Gene Newport', management is defined as the process of planning, organising, actuating, and controlling an organisation's operations in order to achieve coordination of the human and material resources essential in the effective and efficient attainment of objectives. Planning, organising, directing, staffing and controlling are the five basic functions of management that the manager has to perform simultaneously. In addition to this, these functions are interrelated and each one is a function of the other. That is, no function can be complete without the other ones. For example, until planning is not done, organising cannot take place. Similarly, until right kind of staffing is not there, then direction would not be successful.

A detailed explanation of the functions of management is as follows.

(a) *Planning*- Planning implies deciding what work is to be done, who is to do it and how it is to be done. That is, it implies the setting up of goals to be achieved and devising the means for achieving them effectively and efficiently. It is the stepping stone for management of any organisation. It is well said idiom that 'well planned is half done'. In addition, planning helps in predicting the situations and choosing the best out of various alternatives to deal with the situation.

(b) *Organizing*- Once the plan is designed, the next step is organising. Organising implies identifying what tasks and resources are required for the execution of the plan. Under organising the duties and tasks are grouped and allotted to different departments, authority is defined and a hierarchical structure is established in the organisation. Proper organisation leads to both effectiveness and efficiency in the organisation.

(c) *Staffing*- Any organisation requires specialised personnel for the accomplishment of the tasks. Staffing implies hiring the right kind of people with the required qualification for the work. Staffing is also known human resource function and includes hiring, training and development of the people.

(d) *Directing*- Directing is a very important function of a manager. It deals with guiding and steering the people working in the office. It includes motivating them in the right direction so that they can put in their best to achieve the goals. Directing has two important aspects- motivation and leadership. Motivation includes setting up of right environment for the work. Leadership on the other hand, implies getting the work done as per the directions of the leader. This is achieved by praising and criticising the work as and when required.

(e) *Controlling*- Once the above functions are done, it is necessary to control and check that the work is moving in the right direction. It involves measuring the actual work against the set standards and the policies. It also ensures that the work is up-to the mark and there is no diversion or errors from the set targets. Controlling also takes care that if there arises any error or discrepancy then, appropriate measures are taken to rectify it. This helps in finally achieving the goals in time, effectively and efficiently.

Thus, we can say that the functions of management are interdependent on each other and the manager performs these functions simultaneously.

Multiple Choice Questions
Question 1 : Which is not a function of management of the following?

(a) planning

(b) staffing

(c) cooperating

(d) controlling

Solution :

Cooperating is not a function of management.

Management is described as the process of planning, organizing, directing and controlling the efforts of organizational members and of using organizational resources to achieve specific goals.

There are mainly five functions of management- planning, organizing, staffing, directing and controlling. For the performance of these interrelated functions, the activities of the various departments, units and individuals must be synchronized. That is, the different departments must cooperate with each other and work in a coordinated manner.

Coordination is the force that binds all the other functions of management. It is the common thread that runs through all activities such as purchase, production, sales, and finance to ensure continuity in the working of the organisation. Coordination is sometimes considered a separate function of management. It is however, the essence of management, for achieving harmony among individual efforts towards the accomplishment of group goals. Each managerial function is an exercise contributing individually to coordination. Coordination is implicit and inherent in all functions of an organisation.

Question 2 : Management is:

a. an art

b. a science

c. both art and science

d. neither

Solution :

Management is both an art and a science.

Art is the skillful and personal application of existing knowledge to achieve desired results. It can be acquired through study, observation and experience. Since art is concerned with personal application of knowledge some kind of ingenuity and creativity is required to practice the basic principles learnt. Management satisfies the following criteria for it to be called an art:

1. Existence of theoretical knowledge

2. Personalised application

3. Based on practice and creativity

Science is a systematized body of knowledge that explains certain general truths or the operation of general laws. As a science, management fulfills the following criteria:

1. Systematized body of knowledge

2. Principles based on experimentation

3. Universal validity

The practice of management is an art. However, managers can work better if their practice is based on the principles of management. These principles constitute the science of management. Management as an art and a science are therefore not mutually exclusive but complement each other.

Question 3 : The following is not an objective of management:

a. earning profits

b. growth of the organisation

c. providing employment

d. policy making

Solution :

Policy making is not an objective of management. It is in fact a process that involves the setting up of goals and objectives for the organisation and the determining the ways to achieve the desired goals. That is, it can be said that policy making is the path through which the objectives of a management i.e. organisational objectives (such as earning profits and growth of the organisation), social objectives (such as providing employment) and personal objectives can be achieved.

Question 4 : Policy formulation is the function of

a. top level managers

b. middle level managers

c. operational management

d. all of the above

Solution :

Policy formulation is the function of the top level managers. They are the ones, responsible for developing the policies and goals for the organization. On the other hand, middle level managers interpret these policies in terms of plans and objectives and works towards implementing them with the help of the operational management. The operational management as per the instructions of the middle management directly oversees the actual work process.

Question 5 : Coordination is

a. function of management

b. the essence of management

c. an objective of management

d. none of the above

Solution :

Coordination is the essence of management. It is neither a function nor an objective of an organisation. Rather, it is intrinsic in all the operations and functions of the management. It is a process through which the activities of various departments and units are synchronized towards the achievement of the common goals of the organisation. It is only through coordination among the different functions of management that the desired goals can be achieved.

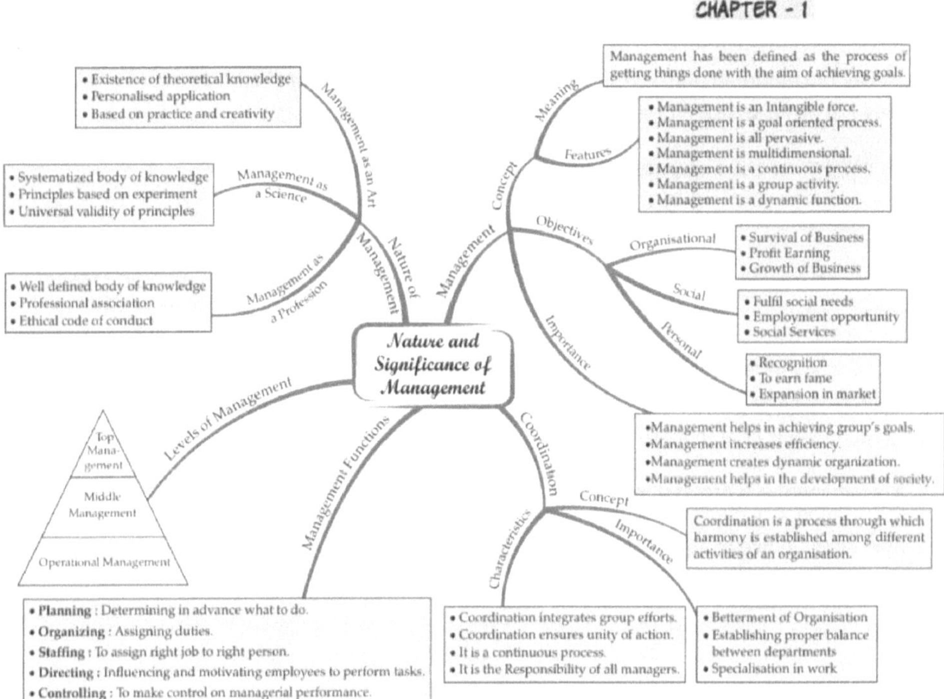

Test-1

Nature and significance of management

Q1. What is meant by management?

Q2. What is meant by effectiveness in management?

Q3. What is meant by management of work?

Q4. List two organizational objectives of management?

Q5. How does management helps in achieving personal objectives?

Q6. Define co-ordination? Explain any two points of its importance in management.

Q7. At what levels of management the managers are responsible for maintaining the quality of output and safety standards?

Q8. Your grandfather has retired from an organization in which he is responsible for implementing the plans developed by the top management. At which level of management was he working? State the functions performed at this level.

Q9. Identify the nature of management when it is practiced as personal application of existing knowledge to achieve desired results.

Q10. Co-ordination is the essence of management. Clarify this point of view.

Q11. Management is not visible, it can be felt. Explain.

Q12. Explain in brief management as a group of people having managerial responsibility for an enterprise.

Q13. Is there any difference in planning, organizing, directing, staffing and controlling of various organizations such as school, a club, a restaurant and a steel plant? To which characteristic of management is this case related?

Q14. Management is a profession. Do you agree? Give reasons.

Q15. Interdependence of different processes is one point of the importance of coordination. Clarify.

Test-2

Nature and significance of management

Q1.what is meant by management of people?

Q2. What do you mean by personal objectives of management?

Q3. List two social objectives of management?

Q4. What is meant by efficiency in management?

Q5. Explain any five features of co-ordination?

Q6. At what levels of management the managers are responsible for the welfare and survival of the organization?

Q7. Identify the nature of management when it is said to be a systematized body of knowledge and explain certain general truths.

Q8. Your grandfather has retires as a Director of a manufacturing company. At which level of management was he working? State the various functions performed at this level.

Q9. Explain in brief management as a dynamic function?

Q10. How does management helps in development of society?

Q11. Clarify how management possesses the feature of art namely personalized application?

Q12. What does pyramid form of levels of management indicate?

Q13. Clarify that coordination does not get established spontaneously.

Q14. Management is a series of continuous interrelated functions. Comment.

Q15. Anything minus management is nothing. What does this statement tell? Explain.

Test-3

Nature and significance of management

Q1. Why coordination is called essence of management?

Q2. Name the level of management at which the managers are responsible for implementing and controlling the plans and strategies of the organization.

Q3. The principles of management are different from those used in pure science. Write any one difference.

Q4. Explain by giving four points why management is important in any organization.

Q5. Your uncle is working as a marketing manager. At what level of management is he working and state any four functions performed by him?

Q6. Volvo ltd has a target of producing 10000 shirts at a cost of 100 each. The production manager achieves this target at a cost of 90 per shirt. Do you think production manager is effective or efficient?

Q7. Management is multidimensional. Explain?

Q8. Coordination is needed for all functions of management. Do you agree with this statement? Give reasons in support of your answer.

Q9. Management is considered as both art and science. Explain .

Q10. Explain in brief management as a process?

Q11. How is management goal oriented process?

Q12. Explain any five features of coordination?

Q13. Explain in brief the functions of lower levels of management?

Q14. Explain in brief importance of management?

Q15. Explain management is multidimensional?

Test-4

Nature and significance of management

Q1. To make time table in an educational institution is an example of coordination. Comment.

Q2. Why management is not called a perfect science?

Q3. Anything minus management is nothing. Here what is the meaning of anything and nothing

Q4. Nothing is permanent in management. Give an example.

Q5. You have three brothers. They are working in three different MNCs as general manager, supervisor and deputy personnel manager. What functions of management do you think they are performing in their companies? Are they performing the same functions of management? If yes, how?

Q6. Explain how does coordination integrates group efforts and ensure unity of action?

Q7. How is management continuous process?

Q8. Is management a profession on the basis of ethical code of conduct?

Q9. Name any two designations and two functions given to first line of managers?

Q10. How is coordination a continuous process?

Q11. What function does a representative professional association perform?

Q12. Why is it said that management is all pervasive?

Q13. Why is it said that management is a goal oriented process?

Q14. Discuss the social objectives of management?

Q15. How does management helps in achieving personal objectives?

Test Paper-5

Q.1 Match the columns:

(i) The force that binds all the other functions of management	(A) Planning
(ii) Doing the right task, completing activities and achieving goals.	(B) Coordination
(iii) Doing the task correctly and with minimum cost.	(C) Efficiency
(iv) Setting goals and developing a way of achieving them efficiently and effectively.	(D) Effectiveness

Q.2 Management is

(a) A Science (b) An Art (c) both science and art (d) Neither

Q.3 A firm plans in advance and has a sound organization structure with efficient supervisory staff and control system but on several occasion it finds that plans are not being adhered to. It leads to confusion and duplication of work. Advise remedy.

Q.4 It is through the process of ………………that a manager ensure the orderly arrangement of individual and group efforts to ensure unity of action in the realisation of common objectives.

Q.5 Justify how coordination is (a) a continuous process (b) an all-pervasive function.

Q.6 Mita has a successful ice cream business at Bikaner, namely 'Smartflavours. Her ice creams are utterly delicious. She makes ice creams from fresh milk and the same are available in a wide range of flavours and packs. She sets viable business objectives and works with the same in mind in order to ensure that the customers will come back for purchasing. Having the first mover advantage. her business was doing well. To earn higher profits, she started cutting down costs. This would sometimes lead to delay in delivery and the ice cream was not reaching the market in time. Over a period of time, the demand for her ice cream declined and because of it the competitors entered the market. She lost some of her market share to competitors. At the beginning of summer season, she got back to back orders for supply of 4,000 ice cream packs of different flavours for special occasions. To ensure that the task was completed and orders delivered in time she hired additional workers. She was, thus able to produce and deliver the ice cream packs but at a high production cost. While completing activities and finishing the given task for achieving goals, Mita realised that she was ignoring one of the important aspects of management. Identify the aspect of management that has been ignored by Mita.

Also explain the same with the help of an example.

0.7 Successful organizations do not achieve their goals by chance but by following a deliberate process. and explain its importance by giving any three points

Q-8 "Management seeks to achieve certain objectives which must be derived from the basic purpose of the business In the light of this statement explain the objectives of management.

Q.9 Forex Ltd. is a private limited company with several branches all over India. It promores the sales of Indian handloom and handicraft products while providing equitable employment to traditional artisans Mr. Brijesh. a branch manager of the company plans his winter collection in the month of June itself. He has to ensure that there is adequate workforce and continuously monitor whether production is proceeding according to plans. He also provides direction and motivation to his employees. The purchase, production and sales departmental efforts are coordinated by Mr. Brijesh for achieving organisational objectives harmoniously. sales department coordinate their work, so that production takes place according to the demand in the market. The purchase department is responsible for procuring material. This then becomes the basis of the activities of the production department and finally sales can take place.

a. Identify any three functions of management performed by Mr. Brijesh in Forex Ltd. by quoting lines from the above case

b. Identify and explain any two features of coordination discussed in the above case

<u>Test 6</u>

1. Management has to see what tasks are completed and goals are achieved with the least amount of resource at a minimum cost. Identify by quoting lines the two important aspects of the concept of management highlighted in the statement.
2. ……………………… gives common flows to group effort to ensure that performance is as it was planned and scheduled.
3. Through ………………….the management helps individuals to develop team spirit, cooperation and commitment.
4. Das is the Managing Director of Gamut Ltd., manufacturing different varieties of cheese. He has an team working under him consisting of Rajat, the Production manager, Vinay - the Marketing manager the Finance manager. They understand and interpret the policies made by Das, ensure that their departments have adequate manpower, assign them the necessary duties and

motivate them to achieve the desired objectives. State one more function other than those mentioned above, that his team may perform at the level they are working.

5. Indian Railways has launched a new broad gauge solar power train which is going to be a path breaking leap towards making trains greener and more environment friendly. The solar power DEMU (Diesel Electric Multiple Unit) has 6 trailer coaches and is expressed to save about 21,000 liters of diesel and ensuring a cost saving of 12,00,000 per year. Identify and explain the objectives of management achieved by Indian Railways in the above case

6. The management of Vrinda Lady Only believes that the members of an organization should work towards fulfilling the common organizational goal. This requires team work and integration of efforts of all individuals and departments and specialists .This is because all the individuals and departments depend on each other for information and resources to perform their respective activities. Managers need to reconcile differences in approach, timing, efforts or interest. At the same time it should enable all its members to grow and develop. Thus, there is a need to harmonize individual goals and organizational goals. Identify and plain the concept of management discussed above

   State the characteristic of management which is reflected from the above para

7. Science is a systematized body of knowledge that explains certain general truths or the operation laws" In the light of this statement, describe whether management is a science.

8. "Coordination is the orderly arrangement of group efforts to provide unity of action in the pursuit of common purpose. In the light of this statement, explain the nature of coordination.

9. Name the process of designing and maintaining an environment in which individuals working together in groups efficiently accomplish selected aims. Also, plan is importance by giving any five points

<u>Test 7</u>

Q.1 Management is defined as a process of getting things done with the aim of achieving goals effectively and efficiently. "Process in the definition means the primary function or activities that management performs to get things done. Enumerate these functions or activities.

Q.2 The basic objective of any business is

(a) Survival (b) Profit (c) Growth (d) Personal

Q.3 ....is responsible for implementing and controlling plans and strategies developed by the senior most executives of the organization.

Q.4 The purchase, production and sales managers at Sharda Ltd, a firm manufacturing readymade garments are generally at a conflict, as they have their own objectives. Usually each thinks that only they are qualified to evaluate, judge and decide on any matter, according to their professional criteria. Name the concept which will be required by the CEO Mr. Raman, to reconcile the differences in approach, interest or opinion in the organization.

Q.5 List any three tasks that Mr. Armstrong needs to do, as a production manager, in his firm, to carry out the plans laid down by the top managers.

Q.6 In a company, the marketing department's objective is to increase sales by 10 per cent by offering the finance department does not approve of such discounts as it means loss of revenue. These kinds of conflict arise in organizations because of the lack of one of the concepts of manager

(a) Identify and explain the concept of management highlighted above. (b) State the characteristic of management the company is violating.

Q.7 Kamal, Khan and David are partners in a firm engaged in the distribution of dairy products in Ma Kamal is a holder of Senior Secondary School Certificate from Central Board of Secondary E Business Studies as one of his elective subjects. Khan had done his post-graduation in Hindi literature and David in Dairy Farming. One day there was a serious discussion between Khan and David regarding Management as a Science. Khan argued that Management is not a science whereas David was that Management is a science. Kamal intervened and corrected both Khan and David about Management as a Science with the help of his knowledge of Business Studies. Explain how Kamal would have been able to satisfy both Khan and David.

Q.8 "A successful enterprise has to achieve its goals effectively and efficiently." Explain the statement, giving examples.

Q.9 Define management. State any five characteristics of management.

<u>Test-8</u>

1. .... is concerned with the end result
2. Management Is to ensure that the organization makes a profit. Profit is essential for ....
3. Providing basic amenities like schools and creches to employees is an example of .... Objectives of management
4. In an organization, managers need to reconcile differences in approach timing effort or interest At the time, there is a need to harmonies individual goals and organizational goals. State the concept of management highlighted in the above para
5. One of the objectives of management is to consistently create economic value for various constituents of society. Explain the objective of management by giving any two examples
6. Answer the following:
   (a) How does coordination ensure unity of action in Management
   (b) Ar which level of management coordination takes place in an organisation?
   (c) How does Coordination integrate group effort

7. Nishtha is a manager of a company selling laptops. She plans the target sales of 2,000 laptops per month. She allocates necessary resources to carry out the plan. She has six salesmen working under her. She works with them, guiding and motivating them to achieve the target sales. At the end of the month, after comparison of actual sales with the target sales ,she found that actual sales exceeded the target

sales. identity, by quoting the lines from the above paragraph, the functions of management Nishtha is performing. Explain the functions by quoting the lines

8. A company's target production a 5000 units in a year To achieve this target the manager has to operate double shifts due to power failure most of the time. The manager is able to produce 5000 units but at a higher production cost.

a. Is the manager effective and efficient Give reasons

b. Why is it important for a manager to be both effective and efficient? Explain

9. Define management. Do you think management has the characteristics of a full-fledged profession? Give reasons in support of your answer.

Test 9

Q.1 There is a kind of cost benefit analysis and the relationship between inputs and outputs. If by using less resources (i.e. the inputs) more benefits are derived (ie, the outputs), then efficiency has increased

Name any four input resources required to do a particular task.

Q.2 ....is responsible for all the activities of first line managers.

Q.3 Management is required not for itself but for ....

Q.4 In which two functions of management do managers at the top level spend more time than managers at lower level of the organizations?

Q.5 Answer the following:

(a) Why is management a group activity?

(b) How does management increase efficiency?

(c) What is the purpose of coordination?

Q.6 Why is management considered to be a multi-dimensional concept? Explain.

Q.7 Company X is facing a lot of problems these days. It manufactures white goods like washing machines microwave ovens, refrigerators and air conditioners. The company's margins are under pressure and the profit and market share are declining. The production department blames marketing for not meeting sales target and marketing blames production department for producing goods, which are not of good quality meeting customers' expectations. The finance department blames both production and marketing for declining return on investment and bad marketing

What quality of management do you think the company is lacking? Explain its importance by giving any three points.

Q.8 "Coordination is the essence of management." Do you agree? Give reasons.

Q.9 B Ltd. wants to modify its existing product, DVD player in the market due to decreasing sales. State any functions of each level of management to give effect to this decision of the company.

<u>Test 10</u>

Q1. Alia Enterprises, a company was initially producing grinders and mixers. Now, with the changing scenario and emerging trends of working women there is a greater demand for a product which is more efficient and a multi-tasker. On analysing the situation, the company decided to penetrate into the market for producing Food Processor. Which feature of management is highlighted here? Which level of management will take this decision (1)

Q2. How does management help in achieving personal objectives?   [1]

Q3. Ms.Bharti passed her MBBS examination in the first division in 2008 later on in the year 2011 she passed her MS examination as an eye specialist. She was awarded a gold medal in this examination. After completing her studies she joined a big hospital as an eye surgeon. She is performing 10 operations successfully every day. State which aspect of Ms. Bharti's above experience is a science and which one is an art?   [1]

Q4. Shreya is a branch manager at 'Zara', a popular brand of designer clothes. She performs several different tasks in a single day. Sometimes she spends more time in planning a future exhibition and sometimes in sorting an employee's problem.
(a) At what level of management does Shreya work in this organization?
(b) What are the functions performed by Shreya   [3]

Q5. A student of MBA has to give a presentation on management in his class. The main points of his presentation were: "Several representative associations have been set up in India like Bar Council, Medical council and ICAI. Similar organizations have been set up all across the world for management. Like in India All India Management association-AIMA is set up. But in order to become a manager, it is not obligatory to be a member of AIMA. On the basis of the above discussion, explain whether management is a profession. Explain any characteristic of profession on the basis of which management can be called a profession [3]

Q6. 'Coordination is required at top level of the management only '. Comment   [3]

Q7. Gemini Circus is organising shows internationally for the last thirty years. Their shows have been successful across the globe. Of late, their shows are not as popular as they were in the past. After analysing, they are thinking of bringing necessary changes in their shows to gain popularity.
(a) Identify which characteristics of management is reflected in above situation?
(b) Which function of management is indicated here? Explain
(c) Also identify value which the company wants to communicate to the society   [3]

Q9. To save the electricity the government decided to encourage the general public to use LED lights. Seeing the opportunity the directors of Electricals Ltd. decided to manufacture LED bulbs to boost its profits. The management of the company has asked Mr. Simon the production manager to work for long hours to meet the expected growing demand for bulbs in the market. He demanded extra salaries for over time but the company ignored his request.

(a)Name and explain the objective which the management has focused to achieve by quoting the lines

(b)By quoting the line indicate the objective which it has ignored and explain it also.
    [4]

Q10. "A manager is continuously engaged in maintaining an orderly arrangement of his group efforts so that their actions move in the same direction and common purpose of the company can be achieved."

Which concept of management is referred here? Discuss the importance of this concept.   [4]

Q11. Effectiveness and efficiency are two sides of the same coin." Comment.   [5]

Q12. Shiv Nadar, chairman and CEO of HCL attributes the success of the group to its management team and their entrepreneurial spirit which together have enabled it to handle rapid changes in the environment and technologies. At HCL management believes that happy, satisfied and self-motivated employees help in reducing costs and increase productivity. It also has a strong sense of social responsibility and has set up educational institutions in the field of management, engineering, computers etc.

Identify and explain the significance of understanding management by quoting relevant lines from the case study. [6]